First Baptist church

The Ladies' Handbook and Household Assistant

A Manual of Religious and Table Etiquette. A selection of choice recipes.

First Baptist church

The Ladies' Handbook and Household Assistant
A Manual of Religious and Table Etiquette. A selection of choice recipes.

ISBN/EAN: 9783337091552

Printed in Europe, USA, Canada, Australia, Japan

Cover: Foto ©Lupo / pixelio.de

More available books at **www.hansebooks.com**

THE
LADIES' HANDBOOK

AND

HOUSEHOLD ASSISTANT.

A

MANUAL OF RELIGIOUS AND TABLE ETIQUETTE;
A SELECTION OF CHOICE RECIPES FOR
PLAIN AND FANCY COOKING;

AND A COMPEND OF

RULES, TABLES, AND SUGGESTIONS OF
INFINITE VALUE IN EVERY
HOUSEHOLD.

PUBLISHED IN BEHALF OF THE
COVENANT BAND OF THE FIRST BAPTIST CHURCH,
HOOSICK FALLS, N. Y.

FREEMAN & O'NEIL,
CLAREMONT, N. H.,
MANUFACTURERS OF
CHURCH PEWS,

Would respectfully inform all Church organizations that they will cheerfully submit designs and estimates on any work in their line, either for New Churches, or Re-seating old ones. They also Manufacture

Stair Building Goods and Wood Mantels,

Hard Wood Veneered Doors,

and all kinds of first-class Building Trimmings, either in Hard or Soft Wood.

CORRESPONDENCE SOLICITED.

Honestly and Scientifically prepared from the Finest Quality of Drugs obtainable.
Recommended by the Best People in New England.

CELERY COMPOUND CURES.

DISEASES OF THE KIDNEYS, LIVER, STOMACH, and BOWELS,

AND ACTS AS A

BLOOD PURIFIER

AND

TONIC TO THE GENERAL SYSTEM.

CELERY COMPOUND Cures malarial diseases; and to all suffering from any form of complaint caused by malaria, it is specially recommended, inducing a healthy action of the liver, curing biliousness in all its forms.

CELERY COMPOUND Is a nerve tonic which never fails; it strengthens and quiets the nervous system, and promotes regular and quiet sleep.

CELERY COMPOUND Is the best medicine for kidney complaints in the market. It contains all of the best remedies for these diseases, and never fails to cure.

CELERY COMPOUND Immediately relieves and permanently cures habitual constipation, itching piles, sick headache, and all diseases of the stomach and bowels, with none of the evils consequent upon the use of powerful cathartics.

CELERY COMPOUND Strengthens the stomach, and is a tonic and stimulant to the digestive organs, making it one of the best cures known for dyspepsia, indigestion, etc.

CELERY COMPOUND Is never known to fail to relieve and cure rheumatism and neuralgia. In severe and obstinate cases of rheumatism, add one fourth ounce of iodide of potassium to each bottle, then use the medicine faithfully according to directions, and it will cure you.

CELERY COMPOUND Is the safest and best remedy in existence for all the diseases incident to females, as thousands can testify.

CELERY COMPOUND Is prepared by an apothecary who has had thirty-seven years' experience in compounding medicines. Its ingredients are purely vegetable, consisting of roots, herbs, barks, seeds, and flowers, the names of which are given on the label of every bottle. It is the best medicine in the world for aged people, quieting, bracing, and toning the nervous system.

CELERY COMPOUND Is sold at $1.00 per bottle, six bottles for $5.00, and may be obtained of every wholesale and retail druggist in the United States, or of the proprietor. M. K. PAINE, *Windsor, Vt.*

To introduce THE CELERY COMPOUND in places where Dealers do not have it in stock, I will, on receipt of Two Dollars, send two bottles to any address in New England, securely packed, and Express Charges paid to your nearest Express Office.

PREFACE.

The LADIES' HANDBOOK is published in the interest of our Church Society.

The rules of etiquette which it contains are such as are especially applicable to the table, to church worship, and to church observances. Its recipes for cooking have been thoroughly tested by practical housekeepers; they are complete in every detail, plain in expression, and will be easily understood.

The blank pages will be found of value, for the purpose of noting down additional recipes or any interesting events connected with our society. Believing the best interests of the public demand a healthy temperance sentiment, we have abstained from publishing any recipes which contain spirituous liquors, and most earnestly do we ask every Christian mother to guard against building up in her children an appetite for strong drink by the food which she places before them.

It is hoped the publication of this little volume will in a small way further the Gospel interests of our society, and that each one will contribute his mite in aiding the ladies in their good work.

To our many friends and to a generous Christian public it is respectfully dedicated.

FURNITURE. ✻ FURNITURE.

WE FEEL CROWDED.

Business booms, but for all that we still find ourselves too crowded to be comfortable.

ENORMOUS QUANTITIES OF SPRING GOODS

In Stock. We will start them with still further reductions on prices already low.

NOW IS YOUR CHANCE

To capture one of those really great bargains such as are seldom offered in

PARLOR AND CHAMBER

And House Furnishing Goods.

These Goods are as handsome and reliable as any on earth and

All of the Very Latest Styles.

To such good points as these we now add the inducement of PRICES LOWER THAN EVER KNOWN. Who "Takes the Cake?" It may as well be you as anyone else. COME IN. COME IN.

HAUSSLER & SON,

9 CLASSIC STREET, HOOSICK FALLS, N. Y.

J. H. McEACHRON,

Jeweler and Optician,

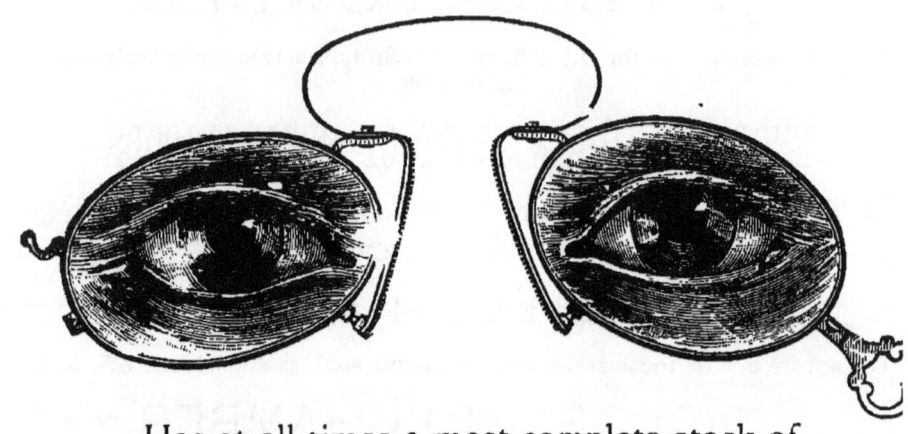

Has at all times a most complete stock of

OPTICAL GOODS,

as well as

Watches, Clocks, Jewelry, Silver Ware, Etc.

And what is of vastly greater importance is that the BEST MEDICAL MEN of the place recommend him as competent to correct all visual defects with properly selected Eye Glasses or Spectacles. He makes no charge for examination and only charges a fair price for fine goods.

You can find him at his new store,

THE PETERS BLOCK.

ETIQUETTE.

The following rules of etiquette are only those which apply to the table and observances in or in behalf of the church. They are classified under their appropriate heads.

ETIQUETTE OF THE DINNER-PARTY.

INVITATIONS AND ANSWERS. — Invitations to a dinner-party are usually issued several days before the appointed time, the length of time being proportionate to the grandeur of the occasion, and varying from two days to two weeks.

The number of guests invited should not be larger than may be easily accommodated, neither should it be too small. From six to twelve persons form a very pleasant party.

All invitations to dinner are issued in the names of the gentleman and lady of the house.

Invitations addressed to persons living in another city or town are sent by mail like ordinary letters;

Written Invitation to Dinner.

> Mr. and Mrs. A. N. White request the pleasure of Mr. and Mrs. C. F. Randall's company, on Wednesday, April eleventh, at five o'clock.
>
> No. 21 Elm Street.

in the same city or neighborhood they are delivered by private messenger.

Ceremonial notes of invitation should bear upon

Written Invitation to Dinner given by an unmarried gentleman.

> Mr. N. P. Leflore requests the pleasure of Mr. R. N. Wilson's company, at dinner, on Tuesday evening, May 20th, at eight o'clock.
>
> Young's Hotel

their envelopes (the inner one, if two are used) only the name and title of person invited. In notes intended for a married couple, it is generally preferable to address the envelope to the wife only;

always remembering that married ladies should be addressed according to the rank of the husband.

Form of Acceptance.

> Mr. and Mrs. C. F. Randall have much pleasure in accepting Mr. and Mrs. A. N. White's kind invitation for Wednesday, April 11th.
>
> Friday, April 6th, 1880.

Dinner invitations should be promptly accepted or declined, that the entertainer may know for how many to provide. Answers should correspond somewhat in style to invitations, and should always be written.

Form of Regret.

> Mr. R. N. Wilson regrets that, owing to a previous engagement, he is unable to accept Mr. N. P. Leflore's kind invitation for Tuesday evening, the 20th instant.
>
> Parker House,
> Saturday, May 7th, 1885.

The answer should be addressed to the person named within it, but the answer to a joint note from a husband and wife, while it should contain a recognition of both, should be addressed on the envelope to the lady alone. When an invitation is declined, it is more courteous to state a reason for declination; if a reason be assigned, it is better that it be real and specific rather than feigned and general. Having accepted an invitation to a dinner-party, a person should not absent himself except for the strongest reasons; these should always be stated in the note of regret.

DRESS. — A person accepting an invitation to a dinner-party must attend in full dress. A gentleman's full dress consists of black dress-coat, black vest, black trousers, white necktie, patent leather boots, and white kid gloves. A dinner dress for a lady should be of silk or other rich material, of the latest make and with long train. A white fan and white kid gloves are also among the requisites essential for the occasion. For an ordinary dinner a demi toilet is all that is required.

PUNCTUALITY. — Be punctual in your attendance at dinner. The proper time for the arrival of a guest is from ten to fifteen minutes before the dinner hour; this will allow proper time for introductions and greetings, and for the assignment of escorts to the table.

RECEPTION OF GUESTS. — The lady who gives a dinner-party should be in the drawing-room some few moments before the guests are expected to arrive. The gentleman and daughters of the house should also be present. The guests should assemble in the drawing-room, the lady of the house advancing to receive each as announced. At formal dinners, a gentleman, on arrival, is handed a tray with cards, among which he finds one bearing his name with that of the lady he is to escort to dinner. Another method of designating escorts is to enclose the card containing the two names in an envelope bearing the address of the gentleman. The gentleman, after greeting the hostess, seeks the lady whose escort he is to be, if she is an acquaintance; if not, he asks the host to introduce him to her. Guests should request an introduction to any members of the family with whom they are not acquainted, and to the guest in whose honor the dinner is given.

ARRANGEMENT OF GUESTS AT THE TABLE. — Guests should be arranged at the table in such a manner as to insure the most general conversation during the meal. Gentlemen and ladies should be intermingled, and gentlemen of the same profession should be placed as far apart as possible to guard against conversation particularly relating to their avocation. Separate husbands and wives, and remove near relatives from one another.

PROCEEDING TO DINNER. — The servant quietly announces dinner by a bow to the host, who at once offers his arm to and leads the way with the oldest lady, or the lady in whose honor the dinner is given, the hostess following last with the most honored gentleman. The host places the lady on his right, the guests find their designated places, and all remain standing until the hostess is seated. Each lady then seats herself at the right of her escort and the gentlemen immediately assume their seats. The host and hostess are always seated at opposite ends of the table. If a clergyman be present, he is invited by the host to say grace; if not, the gentleman of the house does so.

TABLE MANNERS. — In taking your place at the table, assume an easy position, not too far from or too near the table, sit firmly in your chair, and avoid tipping back, drumming, or any other uncouth action. Unfold your napkin and lay it in your lap; never use it in form of bib. Eat soup from the side, never from the end of spoon, holding a piece of bread in the left hand. Cut your food with a knife but convey it to your mouth with a fork. Break your bread, do not bite it; drink from your cup, not from your saucer. When you send your plate away from the table, remove your knife and fork and rest them upon your piece of bread. When you have finished the course place them parallel to each other on your plate, the handles toward your right hand. Eat moderately and slowly. Never cut or break bread into soup or gravy, and never mix food on your plate. Never eat game or chickens with the bones held in the fingers. Never cut pastry with a knife, but always break and eat with a fork. Never put salt upon the tablecloth; bread is the only article of food which may be laid upon the table. Never dip bread into gravy or preserves. Never talk when the mouth is full of food. Never monopolize the conversation or talk or laugh loudly. Never apologize to a waiter for asking for anything.

Never take notice of accidents. Never ask for a second dish, but when passed a second time you may take from it. Never pick the teeth at the table or in the presence of ladies after a meal.

ETIQUETTE OF THE BREAKFAST.

Formal breakfasts — matters of invitation — are ruled like other parties. They may be given at any hour after ten o'clock and sometimes as late as noon. Invitations should be given in writing or by engraved card. They are usually sent out five days prior to the occasion. The form of invitation is similar to that for the dinner-party, but may be much more elaborate. The answer to a breakfast invitation should be made immediately upon its reception. The dress for a breakfast should be simple, — elaborate costumes are in bad taste.

The family or home breakfast may be considered the most charming meal of the day. Each member of the family is expected to be present, no excuse for absence being allowable except for the most urgent reasons. The meal should be a substantial one; the conversation bright and cheerful; each person contributing in his happiest vein to the pleasure of the breakfast hour.

ETIQUETTE OF THE TEA-PARTY.

The least formal, most friendly and enjoyable of all entertainments given at home, is the tea-party. The number of guests invited may vary according to the accommodations which the house affords. Two rooms only are necessary for the company; one for its reception and entertainment, the other for the tea and its concomitants. The meal should not be a sumptuous one; elegant refreshments may however be served on side tables. When the space is limited, the refreshments may be handed around. Ladies must always be provided with seats, gentlemen should be, if possible. The guests should be of one set, or should be introduced in such a manner as to remove all constraint.

One of the chief charms of the tea-party is that it may be arranged at two or three days' notice, thus affording an opportunity of presenting any new comer to your friends in the most informal manner. Note, card or oral invitations are in good form.

ETIQUETTE OF THE CHURCH-FAIR.

Church-fairs differ from other such gatherings for commerce, in the fact that the buyers and sellers are jointly interested in some other purpose above the purchase and sale of goods. Their object is the maintaining and upbuilding of an institution on which rests the whole fabric of society; an institution on which has depended the past, and on which depends not only the present but all that we may hope in that which is to come.

The management of church-fairs usually devolves upon the ladies of the society, and it is they who have charge of the tables and the sale of the goods. As a mark of respect, gentlemen always remain uncovered when dealing with them. Chaffering as to the price appended to an article is wrong, because you can buy or pass without buying. Any unfavorable comment is ungracious to the ladies concerned in preparing or selling the articles for so worthy an object. Urgent entreaties to buy should not be indulged in; people will use their own judgment as to purchasing; their presence is an evidence that they are willing to assist. The disposal of goods by lottery is a part of the machinery of some church-fairs. Under no circumstances are lotteries commendable, and no lady will lend her assistance to this system of money-making. In attending the church-fair gentlemen should provide themselves with such sums of money as they are willing to bestow on the fund, and in all cases their purchases are deserving of thanks.

ETIQUETTE OF CHURCH ATTENDANCE.

The Church beautifully develops that fine spirit of reverence which goes to make up all that is best in etiquette. Etiquette demands that its soul, or Christian feeling, should be kept alive by attendance at its fount, the Christian Church. Manners are minor morals, and nowhere can the soul of etiquette receive higher inspiration than at church. No man can be a gentleman who ignores the charities of church-worship. 'Tis here that a fine spirit of reverence is caught; 'tis here that the best graces which adorn mankind take their rise; here men ascend to higher planes, and acquire those characteristics essential to the true lady and the true gentleman. Attend church regularly; be in good season, so as not to disturb the congregation in their acts of devotion. On arriving at the door of the church, gentlemen reverentially remove their hats and enter the aisle without haste or noise, unless they are strangers, in which case they await the convenience of the usher who will allot them seats. The pew is private property, upon which it is an intrusion to enter uninvited. When a gentleman is escorting a lady to his pew, he walks beside her to the entrance, then steps aside until she has entered, after which he takes his place. The seats nearest the head of the pew should be taken first, to avoid moving along when others enter. It is not in good taste for persons to leave the pew to allow others to pass by them; to avoid disturbance they should remain in the order in which they are first seated. Conversation may be carried on in a low tone before the service, but never after the worship commences. Whispering, laughing, and loud talking are inexcusable. The courtesies of the hour may be exchanged before entering the body of the church, or after the services, but never during the exercises of devotion. In your own church, politely offer your seat to any stranger who may be unattended by the usher, but that duty can be discharged in silence. Whatever act of civility you offer or receive, be silent during service. Gloves will be worn in church by both ladies and gentlemen, unless they are to use holy water or participate in some other church rite. Crowding about the church door when

LADIES' UNDERWEAR.

Gloves, Hosiery, Corsets, Fancy Goods.

Notions Department. Ladies in attendance.

GILLESPIE BROTHERS,

CHEMIST AND DRUGGIST,

CORNER CHURCH AND JOHN STS.,
HOOSICK FALLS, N. Y.,

Proprietor and Manufacturer of

PETERS' VEGETABLE COUGH SYRUP
AND
PETERS' UNIVERSAL PILE SUPPOSITORY.

BLACK GOODS AND SILKS.

At Special Department of

DRESS GOODS AND SUITINGS.

GILLESPIE BROS.,

HOOSICK FALLS, N. Y.

If You Want Good Reliable

Boots, Shoes and Rubbers,

Of Latest Style and Lowest Prices,
call at

MARKSTONE'S,

15 CLASSIC STREET,   Three doors east of Post Office,

HOOSICK FALLS, N. Y.

STEMM & BICKFORD,

MARBLE AND GRANITE WORKS.

ALL KINDS OF

CEMETERY WORK

At Reasonable Prices.

MARBLE AND GRANITE

MONUMENTS & HEADSTONES.

All Orders and Communications by Mail promptly attended to.

Eldredge's New Building, Railroad Avenue, Hoosick Falls, N. Y.

J. C. STEMM.
H. J. BICKFORD.

the congregation is entering or leaving is against etiquette, and a cause of annoyance. Departure from the church should be as slow and noiseless as the act of entering. The church is sacred, and we should there walk as in the presence of the Deity.

ETIQUETTE OF THE WEDDING.

Marriage, the school of the affections, the music of two hearts, ever calls for a joyous celebration. Auspicious hour, when holy love to the altar leads two willing votaries; when love, that pitches man in his best key, or rather keys him to pitches beyond himself, makes roseate two gay horizons. The nuptial day, so calm, so bright, finds its best setting in the wish that the trusting pair may weather all life's storms and grow gray in the kind offices of home. Men are bad in the degree in which they are unfit for wedded life, that seminary of earth's best virtues.

The most fitting place for the performance of the marriage ceremony is at the church; it may take place there, or at the home of the bride.

When the wedding is strictly private, bridesmaids and groomsmen are not required, but when the full ceremonial of the church is observed they are considered necessary. There may be any even number of bridesmaids from two to eight, and the same number of groomsmen. They should be younger than the bride. The bridal dress should be conspicuously plain, and the bride should wear but few ornaments; the bridal costume will, however, be distinguished by the garland and veil. The dresses of the bridesmaids will be of some light, graceful fabric, the principal decoration being flowers. The bridesmaids will assist in dressing the bride, and will receive the company.

The groomsmen receive the clergyman and present him to the bridegroom. The "best man" among the groomsmen will be made treasurer for the occasion by the bridegroom, despatching all the business; will present the white bouquet to the bride, and escort the friends desirous of congratulating the young couple. The bridegroom presents bouquets to the bridesmaids, and pays attention to his young wife. A carriage will be provided by the bridegroom to bring his family and the clergyman to the place appointed for the ceremony. He will, also, provide carriages for the bridesmaids and groomsmen. The parents of the bride will provide carriages for themselves and daughter.

When the wedding is solemnized in church, the front seats near the altar are usually separated from the others by a white ribbon, being reserved for the families and invited friends of the young couple. Ushers, designated by a white rose, wait on arrivals and appoint them to their seats. The ushers in a body receive the bridal party at the vestibule of the church and attend them up the main aisle until they reach the altar rail, when they separate to the right and left and take their places in the rear. Upon the arrival of the bride the clergyman must be near the altar, and the bridegroom and his party should be in the vestry. The bridesmaids may accompany the bride to church in carriages following hers, or they may await her coming and receive her in the vestibule, where the party will form; the "best man" giving escort to the chief bridesmaid, and the others similarly accompanied following in order, with the bridegroom sustaining the mother of the bride, and the father of the bride coming last of all, his daughter on his arm. Arrived at the altar, the bride will take her place at the left of the bridegroom, they joining right hands; the father, who gives away the bride, stands behind the couple, slightly in advance of the others, the mother just behind him. The bridesmaids are grouped to the left, and the groomsmen to the right, of their respective principals. After the ceremony the bridegroom gives his arm to the bride, and moves toward the vestry, followed by the bridal party. As they move slowly down the aisle arm in arm, the "Wedding March" should be played on the organ, and as the carriages containing the bridal party drive away, the church-bells should ring out a joyous peal for two souls made happy.

Receptions of an hour are customary at the home of the bride, and intimate friends avail themselves of the opportunity of congratulating the bridegroom and of expressing their desire for the future happiness of the bride.

Those who are acquainted only with the bridegroom will first address him, and he will introduce them to his bride; those who are not known to the bridegroom will address the bride first, as also will those who are acquainted with both parties. Those who are not acquainted with either, will be presented by the "best-man."

The following invitation to a wedding represents a very fashionable form: —

Mr. and Mrs. E. L. Hanson

invite you to be present at the marriage of their daughter

Caroline,

with

Charles P. Lyford,

Wednesday Evening, November tenth,

at seven o'clock.

Grace M. E. Church,

corner Leonard and Church Streets,

Philadelphia.

ETIQUETTE OF THE FUNERAL.

The last sad offices we pay our loved ones illustrate in a most touching way the covenants and consolations of our holy faith. They bring home to each heart our mutual brotherhood, they evoke those delicate expressions of etiquette known as sympathy, and all the stronger cement those ties which the dark shadow of death has broken. Consolations and expressions of sympathy are the lessons which faith reads to survivors. The consciousness that His help is most near and most ready to succor, bears up the believing Christian in the hour of trial.

The deep distress of the bereaved family renders it desirable that some friend should relieve them of the necessity of transacting the business incidental to the funeral, and from the many painful interviews which at such times are otherwise inevitable. An intimate friend can ascertain and execute the wishes of the family, calling to his aid, if necessary, some professional person, as, for instance, the undertaker employed, who will advise on matters touching the ceremonial.

Ostentation and meanness are equally to be avoided in the outlay and pomp of the funeral, which should be governed by the position and the wishes (if any have been expressed) of the deceased.

Some lady friend should make the purchases

necessary for the family previous to the funeral. The death and the arrangements made for the funeral may be announced in the local press. This will meet the requirements of distant friends, but near and dear friends of the deceased, should be informed by note written on mourning paper.

These notes, unless the distance be too great, should be sent by private messenger. The following is a very pretty form of note: —

Yourself and family are respectfully invited to attend the funeral of James P. Harlan, on Wednesday, Sept. 12, 1880, at two o'clock, P. M., from his late residence, 149 Michigan Avenue, to proceed to Graceland Cemetery.

If the service is not at the house, the name of the church should be given in the note.

Very near relations are exempted by their affliction from attending the funeral, but all others who are notified of the loss should be present.

The pall-bearers should be personal friends of the deceased, and should be notified by letter.

The friend who has charge of the funeral will supervise or send all the invitations, provide the necessary carriages, and instruct the undertaker as to the positions to be allotted to the friends and guests.

While the preparations for the funeral are being made, friends will not call, except to leave cards, make inquiries, and offer services. As soon as the death occurs some sign of bereavement should prevent casual calls; black crape will answer if the deceased be advanced in years, and white ribbon if young and unmarried.

Guests attending a funeral will present themselves at the hour named, not sooner, lest they intrude on the grief of the family. The services may be conducted in the house or in the church; if in the house some near relative, but not a member of the household, will recieve the guests and attend to their comfort. When the services are held in the church, guests will go there from the house. At the church, the coffin will be placed in front of the chancel.

Enter the home of the deceased with head uncovered, and do not resume your hat until you pass into the street. A reverent silence is the best mark of respect in the presence of death.

After the service in the house or church, the clergyman will enter a carriage, preceding the hearse. The carriage next after the hearse contains the nearest relatives, and the others follow in the order of relationship.

The members of the family in passing from the house or church to the carriages, and vice versa, will be escorted by the friend who has charge of the funeral. At the entrance to the cemetery the mourners and guests should dismount; the pall-bearers should remove the coffin from the hearse, and the funeral procession should be formed on foot, in the order observed at the start, every gentleman with head uncovered. The coffin, preceded by the clergyman, should be carried to the newly made grave, where the mourners and guests will stand on either side, while the last sad rites are being performed and until the earth has been cast upon the coffin. Returning from the cemetery each guest will be carried to his residence. When flowers are used to decorate the coffin or room of the dead, they should be white in color. The ornament on the coffin of youth will be a wreath, and on that of a married or elderly person, a cross.

In the solemn presence of death the true Christian realizes the nearness of God and the power and majesty of His mighty hand. Blessed are they that die in the Lord.

MILLINERY.

❖ NEW ✱ GOODS ❖

Are being received daily at

MRS. M. E. DICK'S
Fashionable Millinery Parlors,

GAFFENEY'S BLOCK, CLASSIC STREET, HOOSICK FALLS.

ALL WORK GUARANTEED.

Orders Received for Harman's Dye House.

HENRY W. GEDDES,
PLUMBER, GAS & STEAM FITTER,

ELM STREET, HOOSICK FALLS, N. Y.

PLUMBING, GAS AND STEAM FITTING

In a workmanlike manner, on short notice, at fair prices.

⁌ A FULL STOCK OF

Water Closets, Bath Tubs and Boilers, Galvanized and Plain Fittings, Pipe, etc.,

Kept Constantly on hand.

GILLESPIE BROS.,

LEADING

Dry Goods Dealers,

OF HOOSICK FALLS, N. Y.

Lowest City Prices Maintained.

SATISFACTION GUARANTEED.

DENTISTRY.

In this profession experience is of importance.

DR. E. P. ALDEN

Has made this business a specialty for many years. You may find him at his office in CHENEY BLOCK, HOOSICK FALLS, N. Y.

(Established 1850.)
RELIABLE ✴ CARPENTER ✴ ORGANS.
FOR HOME AND CHAPEL.
Manufactory and Home Office, Brattleboro, Vt., U.S.A.

The Carpenter Organs contain the Celebrated Carpenter Organ Action.

Style 90. [Patent.]

They are pure in tone, perfect in construction, in exact accord with the voice, and full of patented improvements.

More than 50 different styles, ranging in price from $20.00 up.

AN HONEST ORGAN.
(*From the Youth's Companion.*)
"The Carpenter Organs have won for themselves a high reputation for durability and fine musical qualities. An organ may be fine in appearance, but unless it is built honestly in every part it will prove unsatisfactory. Mr. Carpenter makes most emphatically an *honest* organ; and this is, we think, the secret of their popularity."

IMPORTANT NOTICE.
We have discontinued the sale of the "Celebrated Carpenter Actions" to other organ manufacturers, and they can now be obtained only in organs of our manufacture.

WARRANTED FOR 8 YEARS.
Each organ containing the Carpenter Organ Action is warranted to be made in the most skilful manner, of the most perfectly prepared material, and to be, according to its size, capacity, and style, the best instrument possible. Each purchaser is given a Written Guaranty for Eight Years.

TO CHURCHES AND CLERGYMEN we give special discounts, and easy terms of payment. Correspondence solicited.

Where we have no Agent, Organs sold direct on easy payments.

Buy no Organ until you have seen our New Catalogue.

☞ Send for our New Catalogue for 1886. New styles! New Patented Improvements! New Prices!

E. P. CARPENTER CO., Brattleboro, Vt., U.S.A.

N. B. Special Offer for 60 Days.—Write for particulars, and state where you saw this advertisement.

DELICIOUS FOOD, HEALTHFULNESS, AND ECONOMY,

CLEVELAND'S
SUPERIOR
BAKING POWDER,

Manufactured by CLEVELAND BROTHERS, Albany, N. Y., is the PUREST, STRONGEST, MOST HEALTHFUL, and will always be found THE MOST RELIABLE AND MOST ECONOMICAL preparation ever produced for making most delicious, light, white, sweet, and healthful biscuits, cakes, pastry, puddings, etc., and has met with unprecedented success wherever introduced during the past fifteen years.

The public have a right to know what they are using as food. Anything that so vitally affects the health of the family as the daily bread we eat should be free from any suspicion of taint, and housekeepers should demand that manufacturers plainly state all the ingredients of compounds that are used in the preparation of our daily diet. Do not use baking powders whose manufacturers wholly or partly withhold from the public a knowledge of the ingredients from which they are made. CLEVELAND'S SUPERIOR BAKING POWDER is made only of purest Grape Cream of Tartar, Bicarbonate of Soda, and a little wheat flour, — the latter to preserve the strength of the powder. Nothing else whatever is used in its manufacture.

NEW YORK, July 11, 1884.

In analyzing samples of baking powder purchased by myself of a number of grocers in New York City, I find that CLEVELAND'S SUPERIOR BAKING POWDER contains only pure Grape Cream of Tartar, Bicarbonate of Soda, and a small portion of flour.

R. OGDEN DOREMUS, M. D., LL. D.,
Prof. Chemistry and Toxicology in "Bellevue Hospital Medical College";
Prof. Chemistry and Physics in the "College of the City of New York."

RECIPES FOR COOKING.

SOUPS.

SOUP-STOCK. — The shank is the most economical meat for making soup-stock. Have it cut into several pieces, and the bone cracked. Wash and put on to boil in two gallons of cold water; add one spoonful of salt. When it comes to a boil, take off the scum and set the kettle where it will allow the soup to simmer for ten hours. Strain and set away to cool. When cold, skim off all the fat and turn gently into soup kettle, being careful not to turn in any sediment. This will make a fine soup-stock. The meat may be used for hash.

MEAT JELLY. — A nice meat jelly may be made as above, using six quarts of water in place of two gallons.

TOMATO SOUP. — Peel and slice tomatoes enough to fill a two-quart basin (or one quart of canned tomatoes may be used instead); add six quarts of water and two pounds of beef; boil three hours; season with pepper, salt, and a spoonful of butter. Strain and serve with toasted bread.

TOMATO SOUP, NO. 2. — Stew a quart can of tomatoes. Put three pints of milk on to boil, setting basin in which the milk is, into another of hot water. When the milk comes to a boil, stir in one tablespoonful of flour thoroughly mixed with a little cold milk. Let this boil ten minutes; add butter the size of an egg, salt and pepper to taste. Add a pinch of saleratus to the tomatoes, and strain them into the milk. Serve at once. Very nice.

VEGETABLE SOUP. — Cut into strips two inches long, two carrots, two parsnips, one turnip, and a small piece of cabbage. Cover these with water and boil one hour. Strain them into three quarts of soup-stock, and let boil up once. Season with salt and pepper to taste.

BARLEY SOUP. — Boil half a cup of pearl barley in one quart of water for three hours. Add this to three quarts of soup-stock. Bring to a boil and season with pepper and salt.

SAGO SOUP. — Same as barley soup, substituting sago for pearl barley.

VERMICELLI SOUP. — Same as barley soup, substituting vermicelli for pearl barley.

MACARONI SOUP. — Same as barley soup, substituting macaroni for pearl barley.

CHICKEN SOUP. — Set the liquor, in which two or three chickens have been boiled, away to cool. When cold, skim off the fat; then put liquor in soup-kettle with one onion and one half cup of rice. Boil two hours; take out the onion and add some small peices of cold chicken.

POTATO SOUP. — Boil four good-sized potatoes with two onions in two quarts of water till soft.

Rub through a colander and return to the fire; add pepper and salt and two ounces of butter. When it boils throw in a teacup of tapioca, let it simmer fifteen minutes, stirring to make quite clear, then add one and one half pints of milk and let all heat.

OYSTER SOUP.— Mix one quart of milk and one pint of water, and boil for five minutes; add the liquor of the oysters and boil three minutes longer. Then put in one quart of oysters and let boil up once. Season with butter, pepper, and salt, to suit the taste.

PEA SOUP.— Wash one quart of peas and soak over night. Put them, after soaking, in eight quarts of cold water; add one pound of lean salt pork, a small piece of celery, a little pepper, and half an onion; boil gently eight hours. When cooked, it should be smooth and rather mealy. If too thick, add boiling water. If not cooked enough, the thick part will settle and the top will look watery. Have ready six slices of bread toasted brown and cut into pieces an inch square; throw about a dozen of these pieces into a tureen, and send the rest to the table dry. Strain the soup through a sieve, and serve.

IRISH STEW.— Take six good-sized potatoes, two carrots, four onions, and two pounds of veal or lamb. Slice the potatoes, carrots and onions, and cut the meat into medium-sized pieces. Slice one half pound of salt pork in very thin slices, and put a layer of it into the soup-kettle. Put on this a layer of the vegetables, then a layer of meat, then a layer of pork, and so on until all is in the kettle. Put in sufficient water to fill the kettle half way to top of material, cover closely, and cook slowly for two hours. Then add one tablespoonful of flour stirred in one pint of milk, and boil half an hour longer. Garnish the edge of dish in which the stew is served with boiled rice.

FISH AND OYSTERS.

BAKED FISH.— A fish weighing from four to six pounds is a good size to bake. It should be cooked whole to look well. Make a dressing of bread-crumbs, butter, salt, and a little salt pork chopped fine; mix this with one egg; fill the body, sew it up, and lay it in a large dripper; put across it some strips of salt pork to flavor it; put a pint of water and a little salt in the pan; bake an hour and a half; baste frequently. After taking up the fish, thicken the gravy and pour over it.

FISH CHOWDER.— One half pound of salt pork, three pounds of fresh fish (haddock is best), eight good-sized potatoes pared and sliced, one onion pared and sliced, two to three pints of milk, according to quantity required, six or eight toasted crackers. Fry the pork brown, cut the fish in pieces about two inches square, taking out all the bones possible. Remove the pieces of pork and place in the kettle alternate layers of fish, potatoes, and onions, seasoning with salt and pepper. Add water to just cover the last layer; cover the kettle closely, and cook. Put in the milk, heat up and serve, pouring into the tureen over the toasted crackers. Salt codfish may be used for the above chowder, and is preferred by some.

FISH PUDDING. — Two pounds of cold boiled halibut or fresh cod, picked, not chopped up; scald one pint of milk, thicken with flour to a paste, take from the fire and stir in one half pound of butter, one half a grated nutmeg, black and cayenne pepper, and salt; whip in the yolks of four eggs, one by one; put a layer of this into a buttered pudding dish, then a layer of fish, and alternately fill the dish, letting the last layer be fish; put bread-crumbs on top, and bake slowly one hour.

CLAM CHOWDER. — For one peck of clams take six good-sized potatoes, pared and sliced thin, and half an onion, cut into pieces one inch square. Fry quarter of a pound of pork to a nice brown; place the pork and gravy, the potatoes and onions, in your kettle. Shake over the whole one tablespoonful of salt, two of pepper, and half a cup of flour. Strain over this four quarts of the water in which you scalded the clams. Boil fifteen minutes, then add the clams, and four split crackers. Boil ten minutes, and serve.

FISH-BALLS. — Take the fish left from the dinner and chop fine. Pare and boil potatoes, twice the quantity that you have of the fish. Put them into a tray with the fish, mash fine, and make into balls the size of an egg. Flour the outside lightly, put into fat boiling hot, and fry a light brown. The fat should be half lard and half salt pork. Have the slices of pork a nice brown, and serve with the fish-balls.

FISH HASH. — Prepare the fish as for fish-balls; chop fine, cold potatoes, and mix with the fish. Fry brown six good slices of salt pork; take out the pork and turn the hash into the frying pan; add half a cup of boiling water, let this heat slowly, stirring often, then spread smoothly, and brown. When brown, fold it as you would an omelet; dish, and garnish the dish with slices of pork. If pork is objecticnable, use butter in place.

FRIED OYSTERS.—Wash the oysters and drain well; lay them in cracker-crumbs pounded very fine; have ready a spider in which put plenty of butter, and heat until quite hot; this prevents the oysters sticking. Fry until brown, and then turn. The butter will salt them quite enough.

TO SCALLOP OYSTERS. — Open a pint of oysters and put them with their own liquor in a stewpan to heat for five minutes; then take them out, strain liquor, add to it three ounces of butter rolled in flour, and put the oysters in it for five minutes more; butter a scallop-shell and strew it with crumbs of rolled crackers, with thin slices of butter over them, then a layer of oysters, until the dish is filled within one inch of the top; cover it with rolled crackers and thin slices of butter, and pour liquor over; then brown in an oven, and serve. Seasoning may be added if preferred, but most epicures like the natural taste of the oyster.

SCALLOPED OYSTERS. — Butter a baking-dish, and sprinkle a layer of cracker crumbs over the bottom; warm the oysters very slightly in their own

1880. 　　　　　　　　　　　　　　　　　1887.

CLOTHING, GENTS' FURNISHINGS,
BOOTS AND SHOES.
A. ABRAM

Informs the public in general that he has received his full stock of SPRING AND SUMMER GOODS, and is now ready for inspection. Prices ranging from the cheapest to the best, and satisfaction guaranteed. Give him an early call.

MERCHANT TAILORING

I have in this department a very fine assortment of Cloths, consisting of FOREIGN AND DOMESTIC GOODS, and only for Custom Work. A first-class fit guaranteed every time.

A call will be thoroughly appreciated.

A. ABRAM,
SHERIDAN'S BLOCK, COR. MAIN AND JOHN STS., HOOSICK FALLS.

JOSEPH BUCKLEY,
DEALER IN
GROCERIES, PROVISIONS,
AND
C=O=A=L.

OFFICE AND STORE, OPPOSITE TROY & BOSTON PASSENGER DEPOT, HOOSICK FALLS.

JOSEPH BUCKLEY.

Orders received by Telephone.

E. P. MARKHAM,
DEALER IN
STAPLE AND FANCY DRY GOODS.

Well Selected Lines of

Laces, Hamburgs, Gloves, Dress Trimmings, Buttons, and all kinds of Notions.

COMPLETE * STOCK * OF * GROCERIES,
CANNED GOODS,
HATS, CAPS, BOOTS, SHOES,
CROCKERY, &c., &c.

MY MOTTO: THE BEST GOODS FOR THE LEAST MONEY.

E. P. MARKHAM,
COR. CHURCH AND RIVER STS.,   HOOSICK FALLS, N. Y.

GO TO
STONE, * THE * DRUGGIST,

For everything useful and necessary in the Springtime.

INSECT POWDER, CAMPHOR GUM AND Carbolized Paper for putting away Furs.

DYE STUFFS.   GARDEN AND FLOWER SEED.

PURE GROUND SPICES.

CREAM TARTAR, BI-CARBONATE SODA, &c., in bulk.

POTASH Concentrated and by weight, and everything usually kept in a retail drug store, at prices that cannot fail to satisfy all.

HENRY W. STONE,
8 JOHN STREET,   -   -   -   HOOSICK FALLS, N. Y.

liquor, then arrange a single layer of them over the crumbs, placing them close together. The juice which clings to each oyster will be sufficient to moisten the cracker, unless you use the latter too liberally. Season with pepper, salt, and a generous allowance of butter cut into small bits; put on another layer of cracker crumbs, then more oysters and seasoning, and continue alternate layers until the dish is full. Make the top layer of cracker crumbs thicker than the intermediate ones. Cover, and bake in a quick oven fifteen minutes; then remove the cover and brown the top. A large dish will require longer cooking. A slow oven and too long cooking will completely ruin them.

BEANS AND OYSTERS. — Boil beans until ready for baking; season plentifully with pepper, salt, butter, and bits of pork if liked; put a layer of beans into a quite deep baking-dish, then a layer of raw oysters, and so on until the dish is nearly full; pour over it a teacupful of the oyster liquor, and bake one hour.

PICKLED OYSTERS. — One quart of best cider vinegar, one ounce of allspice, one half ounce of cinnamon, one ounce of cloves and one ounce of mace; scald all together; when cold put in the oysters; next day scald all together.

MEATS.

ROAST BEEF. — Use sirloin or rib pieces, removing most of the bone; skewer the meat into the shape of a round; dash a cup of boiling water over it on putting it into the oven; if there is much fat upon the upper surface, cover it with a paste of flour and water until it is nearly cooked; baste often; allow about a quarter of an hour to a pound of meat; longer if you prefer it well done.

ROAST BEEF AND YORKSHIRE PUDDING. — Place the roast of beef upon sticks across the dripping pan in the ordinary way. An hour before the beef is done, mix the pudding and pour it into the pan, the drippings from the beef falling upon the mixture. When done, cut the pudding, and lay around the meat when dished. If there is much fat in the pan before the pudding is ready, drain it off, leaving just enough to prevent the batter from sticking.

YORKSHIRE PUDDING. — One pint of milk, four eggs beaten separately, two cups of flour and one teaspoonful of salt. Be careful and not get the batter too stiff.

SPICED BEEF. — Take a piece of beef from the forequarter weighing ten pounds. Those who like fat should select a fatty piece; those who prefer lean may take the shoulder clod, or upper part of the fore leg. Take one pint of salt, one teacupful of molasses or brown sugar, one tablespoonful each of ground cloves, allspice and pepper, and two tablespoonfuls of pulverized saltpetre. Place the beef in a deep pan; rub with this mixture. Turn and rub each side twice a day for a week. Then wash off the spices; put in a pot of boiling water, and, as often as it boils hard, turn in a teacupful of cold water. It must simmer for five hours on the back of the stove. When cold, press under a heavy weight, and you will never desire to buy corned beef of the butcher again. Your pickle will do for another ten pounds of beef, first rubbing into it a handful of salt. It can be renewed, and a piece kept in preparation every day.

MEAT BALLS. — Take any bits of cold meat, add one onion, and chop fine. Mix with one egg a few bread-crumbs and a spoonful of flour; season with pepper and salt, and moisten with a little water or cold gravy. Mix it with the meat, make into small balls, roll in flour, and fry quite brown.

STEAMED SAUSAGE — FOR TEA. — Lay a roll of sausage in a deep plate in the steamer; steam three hours; then remove from the plate, which will be filled with fat. When cold, slice thin.

VEAL CUTLETS. — Trim the slices of veal; salt; and dip into a beaten egg, and then into rolled cracker-crumbs, or bread-crumbs rubbed fine. Have in your fryingpan a tablespoonful of lard, very hot, into which put the cutlet, and let it cook slowly on the back of the stove, frequently turning so that the whole will be a golden brown when done. Halibut steak can be cooked in the same manner.

BROILED BEEFSTEAK. — Cut the steak about three-quarters of an inch thick. Have a clear fire, lay the steak on the gridiron, and dredge it lightly with flour. Cook the steak ten minutes, if you desire it rare; fifteen minutes, if you wish it well done. Season with butter, pepper, and salt, and serve in a hot dish at once. Never pound steak before cooking.

BEEFSTEAK SMOTHERED IN ONIONS. — Fry brown four slices of salt pork; take out the pork, and put in six onions, sliced thin. Fry about ten minutes, stirring all the while; then take out all except a thin layer, and upon this lay a slice of steak, then a layer of onions, then steak, and cover thick with onions. Dredge each layer with pepper, salt, and flour. Pour over this one cupful of boiling water, and cover tight. Simmer half an hour.

FLANK ROAST, STUFFED. — Prepare a dressing, same as for roast turkey. Spread this over flank of beef, about three-fourths of an inch thick; roll, and secure with twine. Roast same as beef, and slice thin. Cheap and very nice.

DRIED BEEF. — Cut in very thin slices. Place them in a pan and cover well with tepid water; let it gradually boil, then pour off the water. Sprinkle the beef with pepper and butter, which let melt and boil for a minute. You may add beaten eggs, or cream and flour worked well together. It may be served on thin slices of toast which has been dipped in boiling water with a little salt in it.

VEAL PATTIES. — Three and a half pounds of veal, six small crackers, one tablespoonful of salt, one teaspoonful of pepper, one nutmeg, one slice of pork chopped with the veal and a piece of butter the size of an egg: roll the cracker fine. Mix with the spices and meat. Make into a loaf, like bread; put bits of butter and grated bread-crumbs on the top. Put it into a pan with a little water. Baste frequently while baking; bake two hours. To be eaten cold.

HARICOT OF MUTTON. — Take cold mutton (boiled or roasted), cut into slices and lay in a deep saucepan; then put in, one-fourth of an onion, the same of turnip, two potatoes, and one carrot, all cut in small pieces. Dredge with flour, salt, and pepper. Cover with cold water and boil for one hour; then add two spoonfuls of flour mixed with cold water, and boil one hour longer. Have a dish with an edging of mashed potatoes, and into the centre turn the haricot.

VEAL CUTLETS. — Fry brown, eight slices of salt pork. Take them up, and to the fat add two large spoonfuls of lard. Have ready thin slices of veal; dip them in a well-beaten egg, then into crackercrumbs, and fry a nice brown. Season the meat before dipping with pepper and salt. Serve with the salt pork.

A-LA-MODE BEEF. — Take six pounds of the round of beef, cut deep gashes in it, and rub in, a handful of salt, a spoonful of cinnamon, half a spoonful each of clove and allspice, one of mace, one of pepper, and a half-cup of flour. Fill the gashes with a dressing made as for turkey, adding a little chopped onion. Sew the gashes together, and bind the beef with strips of cloth. Lay the beef into a small kettle, put in a whole onion, add cold water enough to cover, and simmer three hours. Make a thickening with four spoonfuls of flour, and stir in. At the same time stir in two spoonfuls of mushroom or walnut catsup, and simmer one hour longer.

FRIED LIVER. — Cut either beef or pork liver

into slices about half an inch thick; pour boiling water over them, and let them stand twenty minutes; drain and dredge with flour, salt and pepper. Fry six slices of salt pork brown; take them up, and in the fat fry the liver fifteen minutes. Serve with the pork.

FRIED TRIPE. — Cut the tripe into handsome squares, and dredge with salt, pepper and flour, and fry a light brown in either drippings or lard.

TO ROAST A TURKEY. — When nicely washed and drained, fill both breast and body with a dressing prepared thus: To one-fourth of a pound of salt pork chopped fine, add one quart of bread-crumbs. Season with salt, pepper and sage; add one gill of milk. Boil the giblets until quite tender, chop fine and add about one half to the dressing, reserving the remainder for the gravy. Add enough of the water in which the giblets are boiled to make the dressing quite moist. Sew up the breast and body, and tie the wings and legs close to the body. Rub over with butter and salt. Bake a common sized turkey four hours in a slow oven. Baste with drippings frequently.

ROAST TURKEY, WITH OYSTERS. — After drawing the turkey, rinse with soda and water, and then with clear water. Prepare a dressing of bread-crumbs, mixed with butter, pepper, salt, and sage; wet with hot water or milk; add the yolks of two eggs; mince a dozen oysters and stir into dressing. Fill the turkey with this, and sew it up with strong thread. Dredge it with flour before roasting, and baste often, first with butter and water, afterward with the gravy in the pan. Serve with cranberry-sauce, or fry oysters to lay in the dish around the turkey. Or, serve with oyster-sauce made by adding to a cupful of liquor in which the turkey was baked the same quantity of milk and a dozen oysters well seasoned with minced parsley; thicken with flour and a tablespoonful of butter.

CHESTNUT DRESSING FOR TURKEY. — Prepare dressing the same way as given, only leave out the oysters and put in a pint of peeled chestnuts chopped fine.

CHICKEN JELLY. — Joint two chickens, as for fricassee; leave out the giblets, take off the skin, boil in water enough to cover, until all the bones can be easily removed. Then strain the liquor, of which there must be one quart; season with salt and pepper and a small piece of butter. To this boiling liquor add one box of gelatine dissolved in one pint of cold water; put in the chicken, and after it has all boiled up, turn into moulds to cool. Very nice with celery boiled with the chicken.

CHICKEN, A-LA-MODE. — Put the chicken in just enough cold water to cover it, and boil until the bones easily leave the flesh; separate the meat from the bones, and boil the gravy to a jelly; chop the meat fine; mix it with pepper, salt and spice; boil some eggs hard; slice thin; line a deep dish with them; put in the chicken and gravy; when cold turn on to a dish; to be sliced thin. Nice for tea or for lunch.

FRICASSEE — YOUNG CHICKENS. — After the chickens are cleaned, cut off the wings, and flatten with the rolling pin; do the same with the back and breast (cutting each in two pieces, the back crosswise); clean the giblets nicely, and, having washed all together in cold water slightly salted, put them in a stewpan with just enough water to cover them, or half milk and half water; add a few peppercorns, a little mace and a little salt (a head of young lettuce is an improvement). Cover the stewpan, and let the chicken boil until quite tender; strain off half a pint of the liquor into another saucepan; add half a pint of boiling milk, set it on the fire, stir into it a tablespoonful of butter rolled in flour, and continue to stir until quite smooth; add a little nutmeg; after it is taken off, stir in any kind of flavoring. Arrange the chickens in a deep dish, pour the gravy over them, and send to the table covered.

SALADS AND EGGS.

SALAD DRESSING. — One tablespoonful of mustard, one of sugar, one teaspoonful of salt, one-tenth teaspoonful of cayenne pepper and the yolks of three uncooked eggs. Put this mixture in an earthen dish; set on ice, and stir with a silver or wooden spoon until it is well mixed, then add very gradually one bottle of table oil. Stir until very light; then stir in half a cup of vinegar. Stir one way all the time. A cup of whipped cream stirred in, the last thing, is a great addition.

E. K. McLEAN, 21 CHURCH ST.,

—DEALER IN—

STOVES,
RANGES
AND
FURNACES.
TIN,
HOLLOW
AND
WOODEN
WARE,
PUMPS.
SINKS,

IRON and
LEAD
PIPE.
BATH TUBS,
BOILERS,
WASH BOWLS
AND
WATER
CLOSETS.

Also a full line of

Plumbers'
Fittings.

Special Attention given to Water Works Plumbing.

DEAR MADAM:

Allow me to observe that, to be a good cook, you must use everything of the best quality. Now just allow me to say, if you want to find a good quality of Agate-Ware, Tin-Ware, Glass, or anything in Wooden-Ware, just drop into

Parsons' Housefurnishing Goods Store,

and there you will find everything you want to keep house with, from a scouring brick to a baby wagon. **No. 11 Main Street.** Don't forget the place, whatever you do.

Watches, * Clocks * and * Jewelry,

From the Best Manufacturers.

Best Styles and Most Durable Patterns.

Lowest City Prices.

P. M. YOULEN, Practical Watchmaker,
MAIN STREET, HEAD OF JOHN STREET,
HOOSICK FALLS, N. Y.

—AT—

MINER'S CASH STORE,

Can be found a Choice Stock of

Teas, Coffees, Pure Spices, Flour,

Provisions, Green, Dried and Canned Fruits, &c.,

At Prices Very Low for Cash.

Miner's Flavoring Extracts

Are of Very Choice Quality.

Church Societies furnished with Fruits or anything in stock at cost prices.

SALAD DRESSING.—Beat six eggs in a large bowl until very stiff. Add two cups of sweet cream with a teaspoonful of salt, and beat thoroughly. Now add one cup of sharp vinegar, a tablespoonful of mustard and one-half cup of melted butter, and beat again. Mix the mustard in a cup with a little of the vinegar to avoid lumps. Set the bowl into a kettle of water, and boil until the dressing thickens. This will keep for weeks.

CHICKEN SALAD.—Boil tender, four good-sized chickens; when cold, cut off the white meat and chop rather coarse. Cut off the white part of the celery, and chop in the same manner. To two quarts and a pint of chicken allow one quart and a pint of the celery and a spoonful of salt. Mix well together, and then stir in a part of the dressing. Shape the salad in a flat dish, and pour over it the remainder of the dressing. Garnish with hard-boiled eggs (cut in rings), beets, and the tops of the celery.

LOBSTER SALAD.—Lobster salad is made the same as chicken, using lobster in place of chicken, and lettuce instead of celery.

OYSTER SALAD.—One pint can of cove oysters chopped fine, ten crackers rolled fine, three eggs, one-half teacup of fresh milk, two-thirds teacup of oyster liquid and one half cup of butter. Put all on the fire together and let come to a boil, stirring it well together. Remove from the fire, and add one teacup of vinegar with one teaspoonful of celery salt and one spoonful of mustard stirred into it; pepper, and salt to taste. Serve cold.

VEGETABLE SALAD. — Take equal quantities of cooked beets, turnips, potatoes, and other vegetables if you have them. Cut into small blocks about as large as dice. Lay in a dish, and add celery cut fine; about one-third celery and two-thirds vegetables. Mix with salad dressing. This dish looks very nice on the table, and is very easily and cheaply prepared.

STUFFED EGGS. — Boil eggs hard; when cool, remove the shells carefully and cut the eggs in half. Mash the yolks fine, moisten with vinegar, and season with a little butter, pepper, salt, and mustard. Fill the whites with the mixture. Nice for tea, or they make a good relish with a cold-meat dinner.

TO BAKE EGGS. — Put butter, salt and pepper in the bottom of your tin, and then break in your eggs. Bake till the whites seem done. Very nice.

OMELET. — Mix four heaping teaspoonfuls of flour thoroughly in one and one-half cups of milk, and add it to the well beaten yolks of six eggs. Mix this lightly with the whites which have been beaten stiff. Pour into a hot frying-pan well greased with lard — not butter. Cover, and cook rather slowly ten minutes. Cut across the centre, and take out one-half on to a hot platter. Turn the other half out on the first. It is too thick to fold.

OMELET. — Separate the yolks of six eggs from the whites, and beat the yolks thoroughly; add to them one scant tablespoonful of flour mixed smooth in three tablespoonfuls of cold milk, also two tablespoonfuls of butter melted in two-thirds cup of scalded milk; then mix with whites of eggs beaten to a stiff froth, and pour one-half immediately on a hot griddle; cook from five to eight minutes. Double the omelet on the griddle when partly cooked.

OMELETS. — Beat lightly two eggs, and stir in, one spoonful of milk and a pinch of salt. Heat the omelet-pan hot, then put in a little butter; when melted turn in the beaten eggs; set on the fire, shake the pan, and cook until a light brown. Fold the omelet, and serve in a hot dish. Ham, mushroom, lobster, chicken, and all kinds of omelets are made by chopping the meat and laying it between the folds of the omelet.

DROPPED EGGS. — Turn a quart of boiling water into a basin with one spoonful of salt. Break the eggs, one at a time, into a saucer; dip one side of the saucer into the water, and let the eggs gently slide into it. Boil gently until set, and serve on toast.

PICKLES.

PICKLED CUCUMBERS. — Take small cucumbers, lay them in a tub, and cover with a boiling brine of one gill of salt to one gallon of water. Let this stand until cold, then put in kettle and boil again, and pour over cucumbers; do this five times, and then turn off and cover with boiling alum-water (one heaping spoonful of alum to one gallon of water). When cold, turn off, boil again, and turn on to cucumbers a second time. Now put a few quarts of good cider vinegar in a porcelain kettle, and when it boils, drop in a few cucumbers and let them boil eight minutes. Pick them out, lay in a stone pot, and cover with good cider vinegar. Use spice according to taste.

CUCUMBERS. — A troublesome but sure way is to cover them with hot brine (not too strong), scalding and pouring it over them for eight successive days. Then wipe the cucumbers very carefully, and put them in good spiced vinegar. Your work is done for a century if need be.

SWEET PICKLES. — Eight pounds of ripe cucumbers, green tomatoes, or watermelon; three pounds brown sugar; cloves, cinnamon, and allspice, each two tablespoonfuls; one teaspoonful of pepper. Spread the fruit with a little salt, and let it stand over night. Drain off the liquor in the morning, and boil until tender in one quart of vinegar. Turn this off, and boil in another quart of vinegar in which are the sugar and spices.

PICCALILLI. — Slice one peck of tomatoes and three good-sized onions. Cover with cold water, and sprinkle over them two cups of salt. Let them stand twelve hours. Drain and rinse several times in cold water. Chop fine, and boil until tender in weak vinegar. Pour off the vinegar, and while hot add two tablespoonfuls each of all kinds of spices, one small box of ground mustard, two cups of grated horse-radish, and six green peppers chopped fine, or two tablespoonfuls of ground pepper. Mix well, and cover with cold vinegar.

TOMATO PICKLES (SOUR). — One gallon of green

CLARK & BAKER BROS.,
CHENEY BLOCK.

FIRST CLASS GROCERIES.

TEAS, COFFES AND SPICES

Are our specialties, and are PURE and the best that can be bought.

In BOOTS, SHOES & RUBBERS

We are carrying the LARGEST, the BEST, and at the MOST REASONABLE PRICES of anyone in town.

BRACKMAN & LEVY,
Leading Clothiers and Hatters,
— DEALERS IN —

Men's, Youths', Boys' and Children's Clothing, Hats and Caps, Gents' Furnishing Goods, Umbrellas, Trunks and Valises at reasonable prices.

BRACKMAN & LEVY,   Cheney Block,   Hoosick Falls.

A CARD.

REMEMBER, **JONES, THE COBBLER,** STILL LIVES

To greet his old friends and patrons who desire dry feet. He'll be found at the corner of FIRST AND CENTER STREETS.

He'll do your Repairing both Cheap and Neat. FOR CASH.

GEO. E. JONES, Hoosick Falls, N. Y.

Established 1866.   Still at the Head in 1887.

HURD & CO.,

SUCCESSORS TO CHAS. Q. ELDREDGE,

Wholesale and Retail Dealers in

Lumber, Wood, Flour, Meal, Feed, Grain, Farm and Garden Seeds, Barbed Wire, Kalsomine, Paints, Oils, Glass, Builders' Hardware and all kinds of Building Material.

———PROPRIETORS OF———

The Hoosick Falls Custom Mills.

To Make GOOD BREAD You Must Use GOOD FLOUR.

We keep only only the Best Grades of

PATENT AND FAMILY FLOUR,

———ALSO———

BUCKWHEAT FLOUR, GRAHAM FLOUR, FINE MEAL, &c.

Come to us for *FLOWER SEED* and Bird Seed.

HURD & CO.,

OFFICE, 4 & 5 CENTER ST.   GRIST MILL, HOOSIC ST.

tomatoes sliced; two tablespoonfuls of salt, one tablespoonful of ground mustard, one tablespoonful of cloves, one tablespoonful of cinnamon, one tablespoonful of black pepper, one tablespoonful of red pepper or four green peppers sliced, one half pint of mustard seed and two quarts of good vinegar. Boil all together fifteen minutes, then pour into jars and cover up. Fit for use in three days.

RED CABBAGE PICKLES. — Take good firm red cabbage; quarter, and take out the hard stalk, then shred fine, and lay in an earthen or wooden bowl with a good sprinkling of salt (about half a teacup to a cabbage). Put in a cool place for twenty-four hours, stirring occasionally; after which rinse in cold water and drain through a colander. To one quart of strong vinegar put, two tablespoonfuls of whole black pepper, same allspice, and one teaspoonful of cloves tied in a bit of muslin; bring to a boil, then put in the cabbage. Let boil ten or twelve minutes, then set off and allow to cool slowly, with cover on. Will be ready for use in two or three days.

TOMATO KETCHUP. — Take one peck of ripe tomatoes, cut or break them into a large porcelain kettle, and set them on the fire. When they have boiled till very soft, pour them into a fine wire sieve, and rub them till only the seeds and skins remain in the sieve. Take the liquor, and into it put, two quarts of vinegar, six tablespoonfuls of salt, two of black pepper, two of mustard, one small teaspoonful of red pepper, and a few pieces of horse-radish root. Put the mixture on a slow fire and let it simmer some three hours. Then remove the horse-radish, and bottle the ketchup while hot. This makes twelve bottles of the ordinary size used for ketchup.

CHILI SAUCE. — Twelve large ripe tomatoes, four red peppers and two large onions chopped fine; add four cups of vinegar, two tablespoonfuls of salt, and two tablespoonfuls of sugar. Boil two hours. Bottle and cork.

PEACH PICKLES. — Seven pounds fruit, three and one-half pounds brown sugar and one pint of vinegar. Put whole spices in vinegar (cinnamon, allspice, cloves, etc.), and boil seven minutes. Put in fruit, and cook until soft.

SWEET PICKLED PEACHES. — To seven pounds of peaches allow three and three-fourths pounds of sugar, one quart of vinegar, two ounces of cloves and two ounces of stick cinnamon or cassia buds. Pare the peaches, and stick one or two cloves into each one. Boil the sugar and vinegar with several sticks of cinnamon for five minutes, then put in the peaches. When cooked till well done and clear, take them out. Boil the syrup, reducing it to nearly half, and pour it over the peaches. Pears and apples may be prepared in the same way.

BREAD, BREAKFAST AND TEA CAKES.

YEAST. — Put one coffee-cup of hops in a saucepan, and upon them pour two quarts of boiling water. Break two baked or boiled potatoes with their jackets on, into the boiling hops, and let the whole boil five minutes. Then strain the whole upon a quart of flour, adding a cup of sugar, two tablespoonfuls of salt, and a teaspoonful of ginger. When milk-warm, add one pint of good yeast; leave in a warm place until well worked. Pour into a jar, and keep in a cool place. Using this yeast, no salt is required in the bread.

DRIED YEAST. — Ten cups of milk-warm water, two cups of fresh butter-milk and two tablespoonfuls of yeast; mix in enough meal to make a thick batter; let it rise in a warm place; add enough meal to make a stiff dough; roll into thin cakes to dry. Use one tablespoonful of dried yeast to one quart of flour. Make up with milk-warm water into loaves of bread, instead of sponge; raise and bake.

EXCELLENT LIGHT BREAD. — Soak two tablespoonfuls of dry hop yeast (or half a cake of compressed yeast) for an hour, in enough warm water to cover it. Then, with flour and a little additional warm water, make about a quart of batter. Let it rise over night; in the summer set it in a cool place, in the winter, near the fire. In the morning sift about as much flour as the batter and a pint of warm water will mix; add salt, and if desirable a little lard; knead until perfectly smooth. In fifteen or twenty minutes knead again diligently. Let it rise until quite light, then knead again well; let it stand a few minutes only, then knead again into small loaves. Do not grease the pan, but always grease each loaf well with sweet lard or butter. Bake in a slow oven; when thoroughly done, take out of the oven and grease the top of the loaf with a little butter; cover the loaves while cooking with a piece of thick paper. After remaining in the pan fifteen minutes, take the loaves out and let them remain a few minutes, right side up. When perfectly cold put away in a tin box. For light rolls, take off a piece of dough after the second kneading, add a little more lard, and bake as directed for the loaves.

WHITE BREAD. — Pour one pint of boiling water into your breadpan; add a piece of butter or lard the size of a walnut, then stir in flour to make a thick dough. Let this stand until cool, then add another pint of water, this time milk-warm, and one cup of yeast; stir in flour sufficient to knead. Put it on the board, knead well, and put back in pan to rise; set in a warm place until it begins to rise, then remove to a cooler one. When it rises to top of pan, stir it down, and it will rise again very quickly; then shape into loaves and set to rise again.

RAISED GRAHAM BREAD. — To five cups of sponge (raised over night for white bread) add one cup of molasses, a little salt, one half teaspoonful of soda, and three and one half cups of Graham flour — or sufficient to make as stiff as brown bread. Raise until as light as white bread.

GRAHAM BREAD. — Two and a half cups of sour milk, one cup of molasses, two and a half teaspoonfuls of soda and a little salt; add Graham flour enough to make a little thicker than cake.

BROWN BREAD, No. 1. — Two and one-half cups of corn meal, one and one-half of rye meal, one-half cup of flour, one cup of molasses, one cup of hot water,

WM. M. ARCHIBALD,
DRUGGIST.

A fine Assortment of Fancy Goods

Always on hand, suitable for Wedding, Birthday and Holiday Presents.

PURE DRUGS AND MEDICINES.

Cigars and Candies.   Pure Cold Soda Water in its season.

Physicians' Prescriptions Carefully Prepared with dispatch.

Store open on Sunday from 9 to 10 A. M. and 5 to 6 P. M.

No. 9 Main Street,   Hoosick Falls, N. Y.

DO YOU WANT THEM?

FINE   GROCERIES

At the Lowest Prices,

BOOTS, SHOES and RUBBERS,

———ALSO———

A * Fine * Assortment * of * Crockery.

IF YOU DO, CALL ON

JOHN KANTZ, THE GROCER,

COR. RIVER AND FIRST STS., HOOSICK FALLS, N. Y.

MRS. A. CORNEAU,

Temple of Fashion,

MILLINERY

Dress Making a Specialty.

36 Classic Street, - - Hoosick Falls, N. Y.

Established 1866.

JAMES WADDELL,

MERCHANT TAILOR.

The Largest Stock of Foreign and Domestic Woolens north of New York.

WILLIS E. HEATON,

Attorney and Counselor at Law,

13 Cheney Block, - - - HOOSICK FALLS, N. Y.

E. R. ESTABROOK,

INSURANCE AGENT

AND PHOTOGRAPHER.

WOOD'S BLOCK,   HOOSICK FALLS, N. Y.

The Best is the Cheapest.

two cups of sweet milk, one teaspoonful of soda, and a little salt. Steam three hours; bake one hour.

STEAMED BROWN BREAD. — Three teacups of Graham flour, four teacups of corn meal, one cup of molasses, one teaspoonful of soda, one teaspoonful of salt, one quart of buttermilk and one tablespoonful of brown sugar; steam six hours.

RAISED BISCUIT. — One quart of milk, three-fourths cup of lard or butter — half and half is a good rule — three-fourths cup of yeast, two tablespoonfuls of white sugar, one teaspoonful of salt and flour to make a soft dough. Mix over night, warming the milk slightly, and melting the lard or butter. In the morning, stir well, and let stand one hour; then roll out into sheets three-fourths of an inch thick; cut into round cakes; set these closely together in a pan; let them rise for twenty minutes, and bake twenty minutes.

PARKER HOUSE ROLLS. — One quart of cold boiled milk, two quarts of flour and one large tablespoonful of lard rubbed into the flour; make a place in the middle of the flour, put in one cupful of yeast and one-half cup of sugar; then add the milk with a little salt; stir and leave till morning; then knead hard and let it have a cool rising; knead down at noon, then again at four o'clock — rolling out for tea. If desired a little shorter, spread butter on, and roll up again before cutting out for tea.

BREAKFAST OR DINNER ROLLS. — Put a piece of butter the size of an egg into a pitcher, and turn on a pint of boiling water; stir it until the butter is melted, then add one pint of cold milk; turn this into the breadpan, add three pints of flour, stir it up, then one-half cake Fleischmann's yeast, two tablespoonfuls of white sugar and one spoonful of salt; stir briskly. Keep adding flour and beating it till it is of a good consistency, smooth and light to the hand; cover it with a cloth. In the morning turn the dough on to the bread-board, knead it well with both hands, and roll it out about an inch thick; cut it in equal bits, as large as you wish the rolls; take the bits between your hands and make them in rolls six inches long and two wide; have the breadpans rubbed with a little butter, lay the rolls in and let them rise an hour; bake twenty minutes. When done, brush them over while hot, with a little butter. The long rolls are nice for breakfast. For dinner, cut with a common sized biscuit cutter.

BAKING-POWDER BISCUITS. — One quart of flour, two teaspoonfuls of baking-powder, a little salt, lard the size of an egg, and enough sweet milk to mix into a soft dough.

BAKING-POWDER BISCUITS, NO. 2. — One quart of flour sifted two or three times, two heaping teaspoonfuls of baking-powder, a pinch of salt, and one tablespoonful of lard mixed thoroughly through the flour. Then pour in one-half pint of cream (or cream and water); do not knead much, but roll out on the board; double the dough and roll again, repeating this once or twice. Do not touch the hands to it any more than necessary; cut into biscuits; make them touch each other in the pan. You will have delicious biscuits with very little trouble.

SODA BISCUITS. — One quart of flour, one heaping tablespoonful of lard, nearly one pint of milk, one even teaspoonful of soda, and two small teaspoonfuls of cream tartar; sift soda and cream tartar thoroughly into the flour, then rub in the lard, and add a little salt. Pour in enough milk to make a soft dough, and mix quickly; roll out half an inch thick, and bake in a quick oven.

BUNNS. — One quart of flour, one pint of warm milk, four tablespoonfuls of butter, and one gill of yeast. Mix, and set them to rise three or four hours. Then add two beaten eggs and one-fourth pound of sugar. Mix this into the dough, and set it to rise about two hours. When very light, make the dough into bunns, and set them close together to rise. When all of a sponge, brush the top with a little milk and molasses mixed. Set in a quick oven and bake fifteen or twenty minutes.

WAFFLES. — One pint of sweet milk, a little salt, a bit of melted butter the size of a butternut, two well-beaten eggs and two tablespoonfuls of yeast; stir in flour enough to make a stiff batter. Rise until morning. When baked in rings, this same rule makes excellent muffins.

RAISED MUFFINS. — One and one-half pints of warm new milk, one egg, two or three spoonfuls of melted butter, and one-half small cup of yeast. Mix with flour enough for soft batter, and set to rise over night. In the morning, dip out this light sponge into the muffin rings without stirring, and bake one-half hour in a hot oven.

BREAKFAST CORN CAKE. — To one pint of sifted corn meal add sweet milk sufficient to make a stiff batter, two tablespoonfuls of yeast, and a little salt; let it stand over night; before baking add one cup of sour milk, soda enough to sweeten the milk, one egg, two tablespoonfuls of sugar, a little flour, and butter half the size of an egg. Bake in a quick oven, and you have a very delicious breakfast cake.

CORN CAKE. — One cup of corn meal, one cup of flour, two tablespoonfuls of sugar, one-half teaspoonful of salt, one teaspoonful of cream tartar, and one-half teaspoonful of soda; mix with sweet milk to the consistency of thin batter; the last thing, add two tablespoonfuls of melted shortening.

CORN ROLLS. — One small cup of sugar, two eggs, one-half cup of butter, two and one-half coffee-cups of sweet milk, one and one-half teaspoonfuls of cream tartar, three-fourths teaspoonful of soda, one-half cup of flour and Indian meal enough to make good batter — not very thick. Bake in roll pans or flat basin. Have hot oven at first.

INDIAN GRIDDLE CAKES. — Take one-half pint of Indian meal, one-half pint of flour, one and one-half pints of sour milk, two eggs, one teaspoonful of soda, and one tablespoonful of sugar. Sift the meal and flour and beat into the sour milk. Sift in the soda and beat again. In five minutes add the salt and sugar. When ready to fry put in the eggs. Graham can be used instead of Indian meal if one prefers.

DOUGHNUTS. — One cup of sugar, three-fourths cup of sweet milk, one egg, one spoonful of butter, one and one-half teaspoonfuls of cream tartar, one-half of soda, and flour to roll out quite soft. Turn frequently while frying, remaining by each kettleful till they are done.

DOUGHNUTS. — One pint of flour, one teaspoonful of cream tartar, one-half teaspoonful of soda, one egg, a little salt, a little cinnamon, one tablespoonful of melted lard, two-thirds of a cup of sugar, and two-thirds of a cup of sweet milk.

THIN FRIED CAKES. — One cup of sweet milk, one cup of sour cream, soda sufficient to sweeten cream, one egg and flour to roll out. Roll thin as a knife-blade. Have lard boiling; throw the cakes into the lard, turn them over, and take out immediately.

BREAKFAST CAKES, NO. 2. — Two cups of rye meal, two cups of flour, one half cup of sugar, one teaspoonful of salt, two teaspoonfuls of cream tartar, one teaspoonful of soda, one egg and two cups of milk. Can be made equally good with sour milk, omitting the cream tartar.

FLANNEL ROLLS. — One cup of sweet milk, the whites of two eggs, two-thirds of a cup of butter, flour to make a thick batter, two tablespoonfuls of sugar, and two teaspoonfuls of baking-powder. Form into rolls, let them rise — then bake.

VIENNA ROLLS. — To one quart of flour add two teaspoonfuls of baking-powder, sift thoroughly, add a little salt, and rub a tablespoonful of lard or butter through the flour; use enough sweet milk to make a soft dough; roll out and cut with a round cutter. Fold over like a turnover, and wet the edges with milk to make them adhere; wash over with milk to give them a gloss. Place in a pan so that they will not touch; bake fifteen or twenty minutes.

VANITIES. — One egg, a little salt and flour to mix very hard; roll very thin; cut in fancy forms. Fry quick in hot lard.

FLOUR GRIDDLE CAKES. — Sift one half pint of flour, add the same measure of sour milk and one half as much more. Beat it well with the flour. Sift in a small teaspoonful of soda and let it work five minutes. Add a pinch of salt and tablespoonful of sugar, and, just before frying, two eggs.

DELICATE GRIDDLE CAKES. — Take buttermilk or sour milk, with one third sweet milk, one egg, a little salt and one scant teaspoonful of soda. Make a thin batter with flour.

BUCKWHEAT CAKES. — One quart of warm water, one large spoonful of Indian meal, scalded, one teaspoonful of salt, four tablespoonfuls of yeast and one large spoonful of molasses; stir in enough buckwheat flour to make a thin batter. Let it rise over night, and in the morning add a pinch of soda. They should be as thin as will turn over, and no more grease used than will keep them from sticking.

PIES AND PUDDINGS.

CREAM PIE. — One cup of sweet cream, one small cup of sugar, one tablespoonful of flour, and the whites of two eggs beaten to a froth; stir all together slightly. Prepare a crust as for custard pie, fill it with this mixture, and bake. Do not send it to the table until it is thoroughly cold.

LEMON PIE. — Two lemons, two cups of sugar, five eggs, two tablespoonfuls of corn starch, and one pint of milk. Grate the lemons, add the juice, and stir together. Scald the corn starch with the milk. This will make two pies. They should be baked in a rich puff paste.

PUFF PASTE. — One pound of flour, three-fourths of a pound of butter, the yolk of one egg, and ice-cold water. Chop one-half of the butter in the flour, then add the beaten yolk, and as much water as is needed to work all into a dough. Roll out thin, and spread on some of the butter; fold closely, buttered side in, and re-roll; repeat until the butter is all used up. Keep in a cool place until you wish to use it.

PASTRY FOR PIES. — Take one-half as much lard as flour, a little salt, and very cold water. Mix the lard very thoroughly with the flour, and add sufficient water to make a stiff batter.

PEACH PIE. — Line a dish or plate with pastry. Pare and stone mellow, juicy peaches enough to fill it. Cover with a cup of sugar, and bake. When the pie is cold, cover it with a frosting made from the whites of two eggs and one tablespoonful of sugar, beaten to a stiff froth.

Cocoanut Pie. — One quart of new milk, the yolks of five eggs, one cup of sugar, the grated rind and juice of one lemon, and one good-sized cocoanut, grated fine. When the pie is baked, spread over the top of it the whites of the eggs, well whipped, with sugar added to suit the taste. Brown slightly.

Pineapple Pie. — A grated pineapple, its weight in sugar, one half its weight in butter, one cup of cream, and five eggs, beaten separately. Cream the butter, sugar, and yolks until very light; then add the cream, pineapple, and whites. Bake with one crust. Eat cold.

Apple Custard Pie. — Peel tart apples, and stew them until soft and nearly dry. Strain them through a colander. For each pie use three beaten eggs and one third of a cup each of butter and sugar; season with nutmeg. Cover with frosting, as in cocoanut pie, and return for a few minutes to the oven.

Apple Custard Pie, No. 2. — Stew apples so soft that they will run through a sieve. To one quart of the stewed apples add two teacups of sugar, one pint of milk, half a cup of butter, five eggs, and the grated peel of one lemon. Bake in puff paste.

Lemon Custard Pie. — Three eggs, one and one-half pints of milk, one teacup of sugar, three tablespoonfuls of flour, and one tablespoonful of extract of lemon. Boil the milk; mix the flour, sugar, and yolks with a little milk, and pour into that which is

FURNITURE.

A Large Stock always to be found at D. H. WRIGHT'S, at prices that can't be beat. A fine new stock of

BABY * CARRIAGES

That are unexcelled for beauty and cheapness, at

WRIGHT'S.

A. C. PARSONS & SON,

—DEALERS IN—

Builders' Hardware

—AND—

House Furnishing Goods.

NO. 11 MAIN STREET, HOOSICK FALLS, N. Y.

DELMONT PUDDING. — Set one quart of milk into water, and let it boil. Add to it the yolks of five eggs, beaten with four tablespoonfuls of corn starch and one cup of sugar. Cook and flavor to taste. Beat the whites of the five eggs with one-half cup of sugar; flavor, and pour over the top. Set in the oven till lightly browned.

SUET PUDDING. — One cup of molasses, one cup of sweet milk, one cup of suet chopped fine, three cups of flour, one teaspoonful of soda, and one cup of raisins. Steam three hours. The sauce for same is made as follows: One large cup of sugar and nearly one-half cup of butter. Cream the butter and sugar, and add one egg, whipped lightly. Beat hard, and add, a spoonful at a time, three tablespoonfuls of boiling water. Set the dish of sauce into another of boiling water, and heat to nearly boiling. Add the juice of one lemon.

SNOW PUDDING. — Dissolve half a box of Cox's gelatine in a pint of boiling water; add the juice of three lemons, sweeten to taste, and let it cool. When nearly cold, add the whites of three eggs, beaten stiff; then pour it into a mould. When ready to serve, whip cream, sweeten it a little, and pour it over the pudding.

COTTAGE PUDDING. — One cup of sugar, two eggs, beaten very light, three tablespoonfuls of melted butter, one teacup of sweet milk, one pint of flour, and two teaspoonfuls of baking-powder. Flavor.

APPLE AND SAGO PUDDING. — Boil one cup of sago with sufficient water to make it clear, but not too thin. Pare and cut up about eight apples; mix them with sugar and nutmeg to taste. Pour over them the sago, and bake one hour. Eat with cream, custard, or sauce.

SNOW PUDDING, NO. 2. — Soak three-fourths of a paper of Cox's gelatine in enough water to cover it, for one hour. Then take one quart of water, two cups of sugar, the juice and rind of two lemons, and the whites of eight eggs. Heat the water and the gelatine; stir in the sugar, the lemon-juice, and the grated lemon-peel; then strain, and let cool. Beat the whites of the eggs to a stiff froth, slowly add the gelatine, and beat the whole to a froth. Pour into a glass dish, and place on ice. Serve with whipped cream. This pudding makes a very handsome dessert.

WEDDING PUDDING. — Four cups of flour, one cup of sweet milk, one cup of molasses, one cup of raisins, one-half cup of butter, one-half cup of currants, one-half cup of citron, spice of all kinds, one egg, and one-half teaspoonful of soda. Steam for three hours. A sauce for same is made as follows: One and one-half cups of sugar, one-half cup of butter, and one egg. Beat for twenty minutes, and steam for five minutes. Then add the juice of one lemon.

APPLE DUMPLING. — Put a thick layer of tart apples, pared and sliced, into a dish, and over them sprinkle a pinch of salt, a little sugar, and a little water. Make a stiff, rich batter, and spread a thick layer of it over the apples; bake to a nice brown.

QUEEN OF PUDDINGS. — One pint of bread-crumbs pounded fine, one quart of milk, one cup of sugar, the yolks of four eggs, beaten thoroughly, the grated rind of one lemon, and a piece of butter the size of an egg. Mix, and bake. Spread on the pudding, after it is baked, a layer of jelly or sweetmeats, and over the whole pour the whites of four eggs whipped with one cup of sugar and the juice of one lemon. Bake for one minute.

FROTH SAUCE. — One cup of powdered sugar, one-third of a cup of butter beaten to a cream, one egg beaten to a froth, one cup of boiling water, and the juice of one lemon.

EGG SAUCE. — Beat together for fifteen minutes two eggs and two cups of sugar; add one cup of whipped cream, and flavor to suit the taste.

STRAWBERRY SAUCE. — Two cups of sugar, one spoonful of butter, and one quart of strawberries. Mix the butter and sugar, mash in the strawberries with a spoon, and stir well together.

CAKE.

WHITE CAKE. — Take the whites of eight eggs, two cups of sugar, one cup of butter, three cups of flour, one-half cup of sweet milk, one-half teaspoonful of soda, and one teaspoonful of cream tartar.

WHITE SPONGE CAKE. — Whites of eleven eggs, one-half tumbler of sifted granulated sugar, one tumbler of sifted flour, one even teaspoonful of cream tartar, and one teaspoonful of extract of vanilla. Sift the flour four times, add the cream tartar, and

Pure Flavoring Extracts

Extracts of Vanilla and Lemon

For Cakes, Puddings and Ice Cream, at

GEO. E. THORPE, DRUGGIST,

CHURCH STREET, HOOSICK FALLS, N. Y.

Proprietor of the "WHOSE-SICK" REMEDIES.

- C. C. C., for Coughs, Colds, &c.
- K. & B., for all Kidney and Bladder Diseases.
- B. P. B., for all Diseases arising from Impure Blood.

THE "WHOSE-SICK" LINIMENT.

J. H. SAVERY,

— DEALER IN —

BEEF, PORK, MUTTON, LAMB, VEAL, SMOKED MEATS,

Poultry, Oysters and Vegetables of all kinds.

MARKET—CORNER FIRST AND CENTER STREETS.

GO TO SIPPERLY'S FOR FINE PHOTOGRAPHS.

A FINE ASSORTMENT OF

ENGRAVINGS, ETCHINGS, &C.,

Constantly on hand.

Also, Picture Frames of all Styles and Sizes.

John A. Sipperly, Photographer.

CLASSIC STREET, HOOSICK FALLS.

PETER COUTTS,

DEALER IN

WATCHES, CLOCKS, JEWELRY AND SILVER WARE.

Watches, Clocks and Jewelry Carefully Repaired.

25 CHURCH STREET, - - HOOSICK FALLS, N. Y.

NEW SPRING GOODS.

All the Latest Styles in

Hats, Flowers, Fancy Trimmings & Ribbons

--AT--

MRS. M. A. MURPHY,

NO. 13 JOHN STREET, - - HOOSICK FALLS, N. Y.

sift again. Thoroughly mix the sugar with the well-beaten whites of the eggs; then add the flour, and last of all the vanilla. The tumbler used should hold two and one-fourth gills.

ROCHESTER JELLY CAKE. — Four eggs, one cup of milk, two cups of sugar, two-thirds of a cup of butter, three cups of flour, one teaspoonful of cream tartar, and one-half teaspoonful of soda. Bake one-half of this in two tins. To the other half add one cup of currants, one-fourth cup of citron, one tablespoonful of molasses, one teaspoonful of cinnamon, one-half teaspoonful of cloves, one-half a nutmeg, one-half teaspoonful of allspice, and a little flour. Bake in two tins, and put with the other half, with jelly or jam between the layers.

PREMIUM WHITE CAKE. — The whites of fourteen eggs, one pound of sugar, one pound of flour, three-fourths of a pound of butter, one-half cup of sweet milk, one teaspoonful of cream tartar, and one-half teaspoonful of soda. Cream the butter and sugar together. Dissolve the soda in the milk. A nice marbled cake may be made from this recipe by adding fruit-coloring to about one-half a cup of this batter. A nice gold cake may be made from this recipe by using the yolks of the eggs in place of the whites, and adding one cup of milk and one-half cup of butter.

ELEGANT CAKE. — Twelve eggs, one pound of flour, one pound of sugar, three-fourths of a pound of butter, one grated cocoanut, one pound of blanched almonds, and three-fourths of a pound of citron.

CHEAP WHITE CAKE.—One-half cup of butter, one cup of sugar, one small cup of milk, two teacups of flour, the whites of three eggs, and one teaspoonful of baking-powder.

JELLY CAKE.—One cup of sugar, a small piece of butter, one cup of milk, two cups of flour, two eggs, one-half teaspoonful of soda, and one teaspoonful of cream tartar. Bake in layers, and spread jelly between them.

SNOW CAKE.—One and one-half cups of sugar, one cup of flour, the whites of ten eggs, and two teaspoonfuls of baking-powder.

FEATHER CAKE.—One-half cup of butter, one cup of sugar, one-half cup of sweet milk, one and one-half cups of flour, one egg, and two teaspoonfuls of baking-powder.

ORANGE CAKE.—Mix well together (without beating) the yolks of two eggs and two cups of sugar; then add the beaten whites. Next add a large spoonful of butter, one cup of sweet milk, three cups of flour, and two teaspoonfuls of baking-powder. Flavor, and bake in jelly-tins. For a filling: Grate the rind of two oranges and one lemon; add the juice of the same, one cup of water, one cup of sugar, and one tablespoonful of corn starch. Boil and cool before using.

HICKORY-NUT CAKE.—Two cups of sugar, three-fourths of a cup of butter, three cups of flour, three teaspoonfuls of baking-powder, three-fourths of a cup of sweet milk, the whites of six eggs, one pint of hickory nuts, and one cup of seeded and chopped raisins well floured.

CURRANT CAKE. — The yolks of eight eggs, two cups of sugar, one cup of butter, one cup of sweet milk, four cups of flour, two teaspoonfuls of baking-powder, and one teaspoonful of cinnamon. Add one pound of currants with the last cup of flour.

VELVET CAKE. — Two cups of sugar, three cups of flour, one-half cup of butter, four eggs, beaten separately, one teacup of cold water, and two teaspoonfuls of baking-powder.

COCOANUT CAKE. — Two well-beaten eggs, two tablespoonfuls of butter, two cups of prepared cocoanut, one cup of sugar, one-half a cup of milk, one teaspoonful of cream tartar, and one-half a teaspoonful of soda. Soak the cocoanut in the milk.

GOLD CAKE. — Two small cups of flour, the yolks of four eggs, one cup of sugar, one-half a cup of butter, one-half a cup of sweet milk, one-half a teaspoonful of soda, and one teaspoonful of cream tartar.

SILVER CAKE. — Two cups of flour, the whites of four eggs, one cup of sugar, one-half cup of sweet milk, one teaspoonful of cream tartar, and one-half a teaspoonful of soda.

CHOCOLATE CAKE. — Two cups of sugar, one cup of butter, one cup of sweet milk, three and one-half cups of flour, three eggs and the yolks of two more, one teaspoonful of cream tartar, and one teaspoonful of soda. Frosting for same: The whites of two eggs, beaten with sugar quite stiff, three tablespoonfuls of grated chocolate, and one teaspoonful of extract of vanilla.

CORN-STARCH CAKE. — The whites of six eggs, one cup of butter, two cups of sugar, one cup of corn starch, one cup of sweet milk, two cups of flour, one teaspoonful of cream tartar, one-half a teaspoonful of soda, and two teaspoonfuls of extract of lemon.

CALVERT PREMIUM CAKE. — Nine eggs, fifteen ounces of sugar, ten ounces of butter, one pound of flour, two-thirds of a teacup of sweet milk, two teaspoonfuls of cream tartar, one scant teaspoonful of soda, and one teaspoonful of extract of vanilla. Put the cream tartar in the flour, and sift three times. Cream the butter and sugar together, and add to the yolks; then add to it alternately the whites and the flour, and last of all the milk, in which the soda has been previously dissolved. Then flavor.

FRUIT CAKE. — One and one-half pounds each of sugar, butter, flour, raisins, and currants; one pound each of prunes and figs, one-half pound of citron, eighteen eggs, one tumbler of sweet cider, two tablespoonfuls each of mace, cloves, and cinnamon; one teaspoonful of soda.

CHEAP SPONGE CAKE. — Three eggs, one cup of sugar, one cup of flour, into which mix one teaspoonful of cream tartar and one-half teaspoonful of soda dissolved in three teaspoonfuls of warm water. The last thing, add one dessert-spoonful of vinegar, stirring briskly. The batter will be very thin.

SUNSHINE CAKE. — The yolks of eleven eggs, two cups of sugar, one cup of butter, one cup of sweet milk, two and one-half cups of flour, one teaspoonful of cream tartar and one-half teaspoonful of soda.

FANCY DISHES.

ICE-CREAM. — One pint of milk, one cup of sugar, one-half cup of flour, two eggs, one quart of cream, and one tablespoonful of any flavoring extract desired. Let the milk come to a boil. Beat the sugar, flour, and eggs together, and stir them into the boiling milk. Cook twenty minutes, stirring often. When cold add another cup of sugar, the flavor, and the cream, and then freeze.

A DISH OF SNOW. — Pare and core very juicy apples, and stew them until soft; strain them through a sieve, and sweeten with powdered sugar. Spread this when cold in a deep glass dish. For every apple allow the white of one egg, beaten to a stiff froth with a tablespoonful of powdered sugar; pour this over the apples, and flavor as desired.

CHARLOTTE RUSSE. — One-half pint of thick cream whipped to a froth, the whites of two eggs beaten to a froth, two spoonfuls of gelatine dissolved in one cup of water; sweeten to taste, and flavor with lemon or vanilla. Put a layer of writing paper over the bottom of a deep dish. Line the dish with one loaf of sponge cake cut into small strips, and pour the cream into the middle of the dish. Let it remain until hard, then turn out of the dish.

ICE-CREAM, No. 2. — One quart of new milk, one quart of cream, four eggs, and three-fourths of a pound of sugar. Boil the milk, and add the eggs and sugar well beaten together. When cold, add the cream and flavoring, and freeze.

LEMON SHERBET. — One gallon of ice water, the juice of twenty lemons, and three pints of sugar. Strain into the freezer, and freeze as you would cream.

ORANGE ICE. — Take the juice of six oranges and the grated rind of three, the juice of two lemons, one pint of sugar, and one pint of water. Steep the rind of the oranges in the juice of the lemons and oranges for half an hour. Strain, mix with the sugar, then with the water, and freeze.

LEMON ICE. — The juice of six lemons and the grated rind of three, the juice and grated rind of one orange, one pint of water, and one pint of sugar. Prepare and freeze as you would orange ice.

STRAWBERRY OR RASPBERRY ICE. — Strain the juice of one quart of berries, and to it add one pint of sugar, the juice of one lemon, and one-half a pint of water. Freeze.

ORANGE JELLY. — One-half box of Cox's gelatine, the juice of four oranges, the juice of two lemons, two cups of sugar, two cups of boiling water, and one cup of cold water. Soak the gelatine in the cold water for one hour, add the boiling water and the juice of the oranges and lemons. Strain, add the sugar, pour into moulds, and place on ice to cool. A very pretty fancy dish may be made by cutting oranges in the shape of baskets, removing the pulp, and filling with the jelly.

LEMON JELLY. — One ounce of gelatine, the juice and grated rind of three lemons, one pound of sugar, and one and one-half pints of boiling water. Dissolve the gelatine in a little cold water. Boil the grated rinds and the thick white skin of the lemons in the water for a few minutes, then add the gelatine and the lemon juice, and strain. Add the juice, and set away to cool.

FRUIT HARLEQUIN. — One pine-apple pared and sliced thin, one quart of strawberries, four oranges sliced thin, and six bananas sliced. Put alternate layers of each fruit in a sauce-dish, sprinkle each layer with sugar, and over the whole squeeze the juice of one lemon. Prepare this dish six or eight hours before serving.

HAMBURG CREAM. — Five eggs, two cups of sugar, and the grated rind of one lemon. Beat the yolks, sugar, and lemon together; cook in hot water about ten minutes; beat the whites to a stiff froth, and mix all together.

WHIPPED CREAM. — Dissolve half a box of Cox's gelatine in a little hot water, and set it away to cool. Sweeten one-half gallon of thick, fresh cream with pulverized sugar, flavor it with vanilla, add the gelatine, and whip with an egg-beater until very stiff.

CHOCOLATE ICE-CREAM. — One quart of cream, one pint of new milk, two cups of sugar, two eggs beaten very light, and five tablespoonfuls of chocolate rubbed smooth in a little milk. Heat the milk almost to boiling, and slowly add it to the beaten egg and sugar. Stir in the chocolate, beat well for three minutes, heat until it thickens, stirring constantly, and set away to cool. When cold, beat in the cream. Freeze.

AMBROSIA. — Eight oranges peeled and sliced, one-half of a grated cocoanut, and one-half cup of powdered sugar. Put a layer of the orange in a glass dish, strew the grated cocoanut over it, and sprinkle lightly with sugar. Fill the dish with successive layers, and serve at once.

FROSTED CURRANTS. — Dip the bunches of currants into the frothed white of eggs mixed with a little cold water. Drain them until nearly dry, and roll in pulverized sugar. Re-roll in the sugar, and lay them upon white paper to dry. Plums and grapes are very nice frosted in the same way.

DO YOU EVER LOSE YOUR TEMPER?

If you do, it is when you have to sift the ashes. Isn't that so? But instead of spoiling your clothes as well as your disposition, you will find it much better to buy

A BLANCHARD ASH SIFTER.

Patented, Oct. 14, 1884.

"Get the Best."

The Blanchard Ash Sifter is a new and most excellent thing. You have only to lift the lid, empty your ashes into the top, shut the cover, and almost before you can set your empty hod down, the ashes will be found in one drawer, and the coal in the other, and your disagreeable work done without any trouble.

It is instantaneous, convenient, simple, cleanly, durable, economical and cheap. It has no crank to turn, or rod to shake. It takes up no more room than a barrel. Any one can operate it who can empty a hod of ashes. The separating is done automatically, as the coal and ashes fall by their own gravity, over a series of grates and chutes placed diagonally in the interior of the Sifter.

Coal dealers say that twenty per cent. of coal is wasted by people who don't sift their ashes. Can you afford to waste nearly a quarter of your coal? This Sifter will pay for itself every winter, and last a lifetime, as it has no wearing or moving parts. If you burn coal, YOU CANNOT AFFORD TO DO WITHOUT ONE.

RETAIL PRICE for Stove size is $5.00; Furnace size $7.50. Extra sizes made to order. Sent *free* anywhere in New England on receipt of retail price.

☞ GUARANTEED TO BE AND DO JUST AS REPRESENTED.

Made only by PORTER BLANCHARD'S SONS, Concord, N. H.

→AGENTS WANTED EVERYWHERE.←

1529 Arch Street, Philad'a, Pa.

A WELL TRIED TREATMENT

FOR CONSUMPTION, ASTHMA, BRONCHITIS, DYSPEPSIA CATARRH, HAY FEVER, HEADACHE, DEBILITY, RHEUMATISM, NEURALGIA, and all Chronic and Nervous Disorders

When "Compound Oxygen" is inhaled, the heart has imparted to it increased vitality. That organ sends forth the blood with more force and less wear to itself; the vital currents leave on their circuit new deposits of vital force in every cell of tissue over which they pass, and return again to the lungs for a new supply. This is a rational explanation of the greatest advance medical science has yet made.

"The Compound Oxygen Treatment," Drs. Starkey & Palen, No. 1529 Arch Street, Philadelphia, have been using for the last sixteen years, is a scientific adjustment of the elements of Oxygen and Nitrogen *magnetized*, and the compound is so condensed and made portable that it is sent all over the world.

DRS. STARKEY & PALEN have the liberty to refer (in proof of their standing as Physicians) to the following named well-known persons who have tried their Treatment:

HON. WILLIAM D. KELLY, Member of Congress, Philadelphia.
REV. VICTOR L. CONRAD, Editor Lutheran Observer, Philadelphia.
REV. CHARLES W. CUSHING, Lockport, N. Y.
HON. WILLIAM PENN NIXON, Editor Inter-Ocean, Chicago, Ill.
JUDGE JOSEPH R. FLANDERS, Temple Court, N. Y.
MRS. MARY A. CATOR, Widow of the late Dr. Harvey Cator, Camden, N. J.
MRS. MARY A. DOUGHTY, Jamaica, Long Island, New York.
MRS. MARY A. LIVERMORE, Melrose, Massachusetts.
JUDGE R. S. VOORHEES, New York City.
MR. GEORGE W. EDWARDS, Owner St. George's Hotel, Philadelphia.
MR. FRANK SIDDALL, Merchant, Philadelphia.
MR. WILLIAM H. WHITELY, Silk Manufacturer, Darby, Philadelphia, Pa.

And many others in every part of the United States.

"*Compound Oxygen—its Mode of Action and Results*," is the title of a brochure of nearly two hundred pages, published by Drs. Starkey & Palen, which gives to all inquirers full information as to this remarkable curative agent and a record of surprising cures in a wide range of chronic cases—many of them after being abandoned to die by other physicians. It will be mailed free to any address on application.

DRS. STARKEY & PALEN,
No. 1529 Arch Street, PHILADELPHIA, PA.

THE LADIES' HANDBOOK.

THE LADIES' HANDBOOK.

RULES, TABLES, AND SUGGESTIONS.

CAPACITY OF VARIOUS CHURCHES.

Church.	City.	Capacity.
St. Peter's	Rome	54,000
Cathedral	Milan	37,000
St. Paul's	Rome	32,000
St. Paul's	London	31,000
St. Petronia	Bologna	26,000
Cathedral	Florence	24,300
Cathedral	Antwerp	24,000
St. John's Lateran	Rome	23,000
St. Sophia's	Constantinople	23,000
Notre Dame	Paris	21,500
Cathedral	Pisa	13,000
Cathedral	Vienna	11,000
Mormon Temple	Salt Lake City	8,000
St. Mark's	Venice	7,500
Spurgeon's Tabernacle	London	6,000
Talmage's Tabernacle	Brooklyn	5,000
St. James' Methodist Church	Montreal	3,000
Plymouth Church	Brooklyn	3,000
Fifth Ave. Presbyterian Church	New York	1,600
St. John's Methodist Church	Brooklyn	1,500
St. Paul's Methodist Church	New York	1,400

WHEN the boiling point of water is reached, a comparatively small amount of heat maintains it. Water boiling violently is no hotter than that which boils moderately. When water reaches the boiling point the fire may be at once reduced. Attention to this fact would save fuel in many culinary operations.

—DEALER IN—

Dry Goods, Groceries,

BOOTS, SHOES,

Ready-Made * Clothing,

HATS AND CAPS,

HARDWARE,

CROCKERY,

WALL*PAPER,*NOTIONS,

Tobacco and Cigars.

ALSO AGENT FOR

H. W. Johns' Asbestos Paints.

HYLAND & BURNS,

14 MAIN STREET, HOOSICK FALLS,

—DEALERS IN—

Choice Groceries, Provisions,

FLOUR OF ALL KINDS,

BOOTS, SHOES & RUBBERS,

FEED AND MEAL.

Will try to please all. Goods delivered to any part of the village.

HENRY W. GEDDES,

Plumber, Gas and Steam Fitter,

ELM STREET, HOOSICK FALLS, N. Y.

PLUMBING, GAS AND STEAM FITTING

In a workmanlike manner, on short notice and at fair prices.

———A FULL STOCK OF———

Water Closets, Bath Tubs and Boilers, Galvanized and Plain Fittings, Pipe, etc.,

Kept Constantly on hand.

TABLE OF WEIGHTS AND MEASURES FOR HOUSEKEEPERS.

1 quart of wheat flour = 1 pound.
1 quart of Indian meal = 1⅛ pounds.
1 quart of soft butter = 1 pound.
1 quart of broken loaf-sugar = 1 pound.
1 quart of powdered white sugar = 1$\frac{1}{16}$ pounds.
1 quart of best brown sugar = 1⅛ pounds.
10 eggs = 1 pound.
1 common-sized tumbler = ½ pint.
1 common-sized teacup = ¼ pint.
1 common-sized wineglass = ⅛ pint.

WASHING FLUID. — One box of refined potash, one ounce of salts of tartar, and two ounces of water of ammonia. Mix and dissolve in one gallon of boiling water. One teacup of this to be used with one-half bar of soap.

COLOGNE WATER. — Cologne spirit one pint, oil of meroli one-half drachm, oil of rosemary one-third drachm, oil of orange two-thirds drachm, oil of cedrat two-thirds drachm, oil of bergamot one-third drachm.

EXTRACT OF LEMON. — Oil of lemon, one ounce; alcohol, one pint; granulated sugar, one ounce; mix all together, and add the grated peel of one lemon. Let stand twenty-four hours, and filter.

LIQUID BLUEING. — Oxalic acid, one-half ounce; soluble Prussian blue, one ounce; water, one quart. Mix thoroughly.

FURNITURE POLISH. — Mix equal parts of boiled

linseed oil and kerosene oil. Apply well with a piece of flannel, and rub well with dry flannel.

SILVER POLISH. — One ounce of whiting, one-half ounce of water of ammonia, two ounces of alcohol, and four ounces of water.

TO BRIGHTEN A ZINC BATH-TUB. — Throw into the tub a handful of salt wet with vinegar, and rub the tub with a flannel cloth.

TOOTH POWDER. — Precipitated chalk one ounce, powdered orris root one-half ounce, powdered camphor one-fourth ounce.

FINGER-NAIL POWDER. — Pure oxide of tin, scented with oil of rosemary and tinted with carmine.

FOR BURNS. — Equal parts of linseed oil and lime water will be found an excellent remedy for burns.

HAIR GLOSS. — Pure glycerine four ounces, alcohol one ounce, oil of jasmine two drachms.

ONE pound of wood charcoal, when burned, will raise from the freezing to the boiling point seventy-three pounds of water; one pound of mineral coal, sixty pounds; and one pound of dry wood, thirty-five pounds.

FROZEN PLANTS may be restored by sprinkling them with cold water and setting them in the dark for twenty-four hours, in a temperature of not more than 50°.

CUT FLOWERS should first be dipped in hot water to wilt, and then placed in cool water to revive them. They will not wilt as soon the second time.

SLEEPLESSNESS may be relieved by laying a wet cloth on the back of the neck, with a dry cloth outside.

THE best temperature for a room is from 65° to 68° Fahrenheit.

TO CAN ALL KINDS OF FRUITS.

All germs of fermentation are destroyed at a temperature of about 160° Fahrenheit. To can fruits so that they will keep perfectly in all temperatures and under all conditions, it is essential that every part of the can and its contents should be brought to a temperature sufficiently high to destroy the germs of ferment, and that the can be hermetically sealed while at this temperature. Boiling water gives us a temperature of 212° Fahrenheit, many degrees higher than that necessary for the destruction of the germ. The use of sugar in the canning of fruits is entirely unnecessary; they keep equally well without it. It may, however, be used at pleasure. With some fruits it assists in retaining the natural flavor. The following method insures the best results. Always use glass cans; use such as may be *easily*, *quickly*, and *securely* covered, and have them thoroughly clean. Place the empty cans and their covers in a vessel of cold water, and heat them to the boiling point. Prepare the fruit, put it into a *porcelain-lined* kettle, heat until it boils up once, remove any scum which may arise, and instantly dip the fruit into the heated cans. Put the filled can, with its cover loosely fitted on, into a vessel of boiling water; the water should come as near to the top of the can as it may and not boil in. Let it boil for three or four minutes that *every part* may be thoroughly heated; seal *immediately*, and remove the can.

If the fruit is not sufficiently succulent, water may be added to it; if very juicy, some of the juice may be removed. This method of canning fruit is much less expensive than where sugar is used, and more fruit may be put in the same number of cans. Where sugar is used, the same method may be employed.

www.ingramcontent.com/pod-product-compliance
Lightning Source LLC
Chambersburg PA
CBHW020859160426
43192CB00007B/1000